The Ultimate GIMP 2.8 Guide

Gimp 2.8 and Nik Collection integration

This book accompanies 'The Ultimate GIMP 2.8 Guide'
e-learning course on www.Udemy.com

The Ultimate GIMP Guide. Learn Professional photo editing.
By Bernard 't Hooft

ISBN-13: 978-1983896910

Printing History:

January 2018: First Edition
May 2018:   Second Edition

CONTENTS

Chapter 1. Install & configure GIMP 2.8

Chapter 2. Working with Layers and color

Chapter 3. Making selections

Chapter 4. Cropping, Resizing, and more

Chapter 5. Google plugins

Chapter 6. Retouching

Chapter 7. Making e-book covers

Chapter 8. Gimp specifics

INDEX

Chapter 1

Install & configure GIMP 2.8

1. Introduction

This book is the printed version of the video course: *The Ultimate GIMP 2.8 Guide* on www.udemy.com.
After making the course, I realised it would be a good idea to also have a printed version of the course. This way you get the best of both worlds.

The book has been printed in black and white to keep the price as low as possible. Although black and white doesn't compromise the learning experience, you will also get a Full Color PDF of the book (it is a download at www.udemy.com).

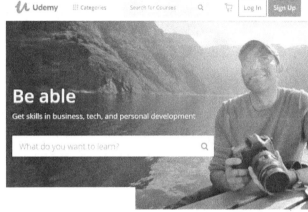

To see the video course, go to *www.udemy.com*. At the right you can sign up to the platform. Then search for Gimp.

Now you see my course. Click on it. At the right, you see at bottom: "Have a coupon?". Click on it.
To get free entrance to the course, type the six digits code: 897371

In the video course you can ask me questions!

Good luck, and I hope to meet you in the discussion board!

2. Installing Gimp 2.8, and setting 'Single-Window Mode'

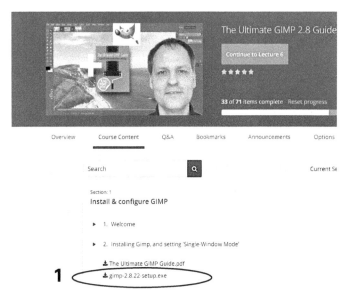

If needed, you can download the latest 2.8 version of Gimp (2.8.22), directly from my course on Udemy.com (1).
The download is about 75 MB.

The installer contains both a *32*-bit and a *64*-bit version of Gimp, and the appropriate version will be *automatically* installed. This means, that if your computer is a bit older, you can still use Gimp 2.8.

To install Gimp, in your Downloads folder double-click on the *gimp-2.8.22-setup.exe* file (2).
Then click on *OK*.

Then click on *Install* (3). Next, click on *Finish* (4).

Gimp can be found under the G in the Apps. Click on it to open Gimp (5).

The first time you start up Gimp, it takes a bit longer.

We now see the default look of Gimp (6).

We start by putting the *floating* windows *together*, to get a single window (7).
To do this, click on: *Windows* (8), and from the drop down menu choose: *Single-Window Mode.*

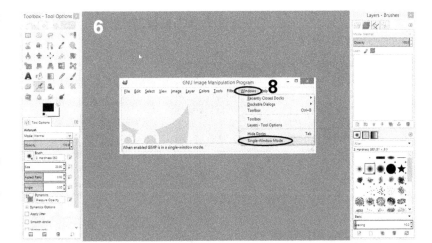

To attach the Gimp program *thumbnail* to your *taskbar* at the bottom (for quick access), *right*-click on the Gimp thumbnail (9) and choose: *Pin this program to taskbar.*
To close Gimp, go to: *File > Quit*, or click on the red close button at the upper right corner.

To open Gimp, you can now click on the (pinned) Gimp thumbnail in the taskbar.

In the next lesson we will install some plugins for Gimp, to change the look of Gimp and expand Gimp's functionality.

3. Installing plugins

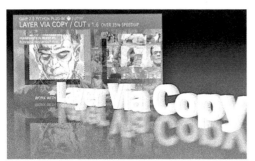

In this lecture we will download and install four plugins, to expand the functionality of Gimp. These plugins are:

Layer-via-copy (p. 77),

Save for web (p. 109),

Resynthesizer (p. 201),

Photoshop Theme (p. 8).

The plugins are explained in detail later.

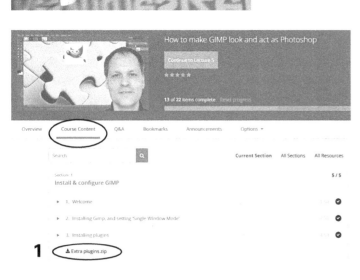

To download the plugins go to *The Ultimate GIMP Guide* on www.udemy.com.

Under the *Course Content* tab, download the *Extra plugins.zip* file (1). Unzip the file.

In the *Extra plugins* folder you will also find, in addition to the four mentioned plugins (2), the: *menurc* and *toolrc* file (p. 7).

Let's have a look at where we are going to place the plugins. On your *C* drive, go to *Users*, and open your *Home directory*. In here is the *.gimp-2.8* folder (3).

When Gimp starts up, the files in this folder determine how Gimp looks like and functions.

We will start by writing a line of code. In the *gimprc* file (4), Gimp's preferences are stored. A particular setting, which makes it easy to place elements to the document edges, can't be set to be the default in Gimp's preferences. So we will do this manually inside the *gimprc* file.

Double-click on the *gimprc* file, and open it with *Wordpad* (5). On the bottom (6), above the text `# end of gimprc`, add the following text (parentheses included):

`(default-snap-to-canvas yes)`

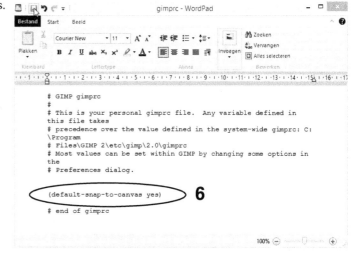

Save the file by pressing *Ctrl-S* (Control key plus S key). Now we will place the content of the *Extra plugins* folder, in the *.gimp-2.8* folder. In the *.gimp-2.8* folder, open the *themes* folder (7). Drag the *CS6 theme* folder from the *Extra plugins* folder, into the *themes* folder from the *.gimp-2.8* folder (8).

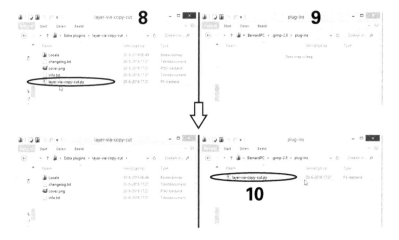

In the *Extra_plugins* folder, open the *layer-via-copy-cut* folder (8). And in the *.gimp-2.8* folder, open the *plug-ins* folder (9). On the bottom of the *layer-via-copy-cut* folder, you find the *layer-via-copy-cut.py* file.

This file goes into the *plug-ins* folder of the *.gimp-2.8* folder (10). Leave the *plug-ins* folder open for some more plug-ins.

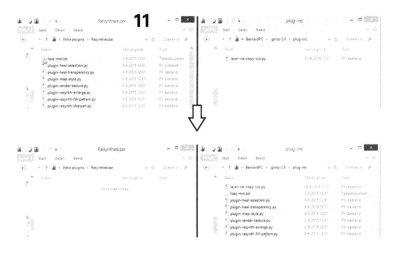

In the *Extra_plugins* folder, now open the *Resynthesizer* folder (11). Select all files,

and then drag them over to the *plug-ins* folder. Leave the *plug-ins* folder open.

In the *Extra_plugins* folder, now open the *save_for_web* folder (12).

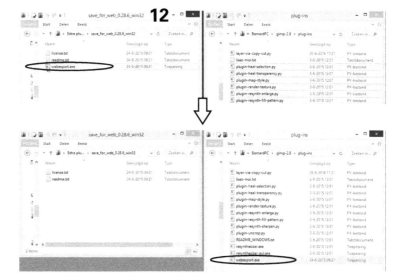

Drag the *webexport.exe* file over to the *plug-ins* folder.

Go back to the content of the *Extra_plugins* folder (13), and the *.gimp-2.8* folder (14). The last two files are the *menurc* and *toolrc* file. Drag them over, and confirm that you want to *replace* the *menurc* and *toolrc* files in the *.gimp-2.8* folder (15).

We have all our plugins installed. Let's open Gimp!

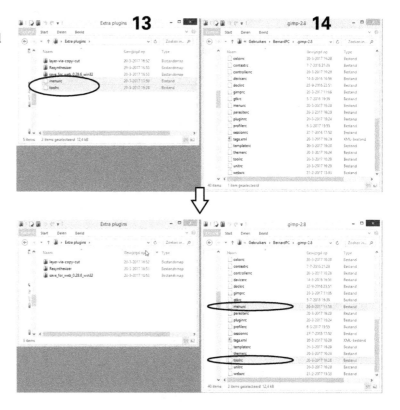

4. Configuring User Interface

In this lecture, we will configure the user interface of Gimp. Open Gimp, and go to: *Edit > Preferences*. Then click on the *Theme* tab. Here we can see the *CS6 theme*, we have placed in the *.gimp-2.8* folder. Click on it, and at the bottom click on OK. To see the theme in action, you have to restart Gimp.

We now see the dark theme. I think it is more comfortable for the eyes, and makes it is easier to concentrate on the image.

The user interface consists of a *menu bar* at the top (1), a *toolbar* at the left (2), and several *panels* at the right (3).

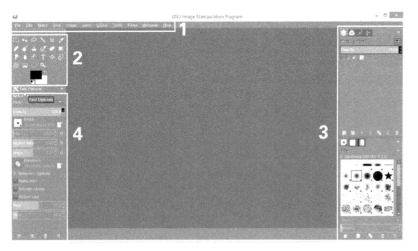

The *Tool Options* panel (4) is a panel that will show you different options for the tool you are currently using. At this moment it is placed below the *toolbar*. I will move the *Tool Options* panel to the right side. This will free up working space because the *toolbar* can then be flattened to the left side.

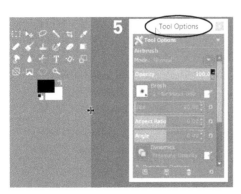

To move the *Tool Options* panel to the left, I click on its tab name, and drag the panel out (5). Now the panel is a *floating* panel. I can place it where I want.

It is also possible to create a whole new column. To create a new column, drag the tab, and when you see a vertical *grey line* appearing (6), release the mouse button. You have now created an extra column (7).

I want however to add the *Tool Options* panel to the lower panel group at the right. So I drag the tab again.

When you see an additional arrow appearing (8), you can release the mouse button. The panel has now been added to the panel group (9).

To see the content of a panel, click on its tab (10).

To change the order of the tabs in the panel group, drag a tab to another position (11).

I will *close* two panels.
To remove the *Patterns* panel from the panel group, I click on it's tab. Then at the right, I click on the *Configure this tab* icon (12). From the drop down menu I choose: *Close tab*.
I also close the *Gradients* panel.

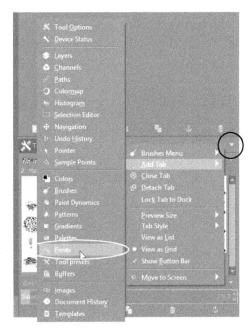

To *add* a new panel, I click on: *Configure this tab*, I go to: *Add Tab*, and choose: *Fonts*.

I will drag the *Undo History* panel (with which you can go back in time, as is discussed

later), from the upper group to the lower group.

I would like most of my tabs to be displayed with *text* instead of an icon. I click on the *Layers* tab, then I click on: *Configure this tab*, click on: *Tab Style*, and choose: *Text*. I also do this for *Channels*, for *Paths*, for the *Tool Options*, and for

Fonts. For the *Brushes* panel and the *Undo History* panel, I will choose: *Icon*.

You can change the *height* of the panel groups by dragging the transition line between them (13), and change the *width* of the panel groups, by dragging at the side (14).

At the left (15), I will drag the *toolbar* to the left, to get maximum space for my images (16).

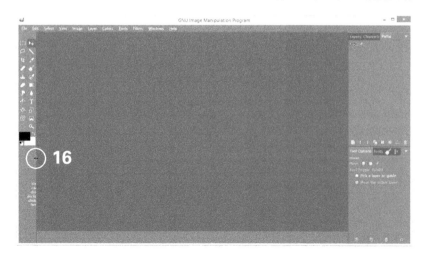

When you select a tool in the *toolbar*, for example the *Move* Tool, the *Tool Options* panel will show several options for that tool. The *Move* tool is for dragging elements to another place. It's shortcut is *V*.

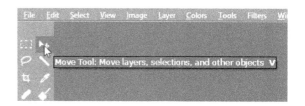

In Photoshop, the default for the *Move* Tool in the *Tool Options* is: *Move the active layer*. It means that when you move a specific element, you can not by accident move another element. To get this behaviour also in Gimp, select this option. The behaviour is further explained in the lesson about layers.

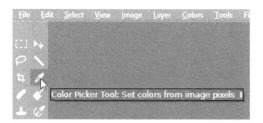

Now select the *Color Picker* Tool. With this tool you can select a color from an image. In the *Tool Options*, activate *Sample average*, and set *Radius* to *5*. Also activate *Sample merged*. These settings are explained in detail later.

The next tool is the *Healing* Tool, which is a retouch tool. Activate *Sample merged* at the bottom. Click at the right of *Alignment* (17), and from the drop down menu, choose: *Aligned* (18).

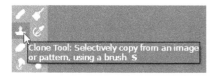

We do the same for the *Clone* Tool; activate *Sample merged*, and set *Alignment* on: *Aligned* (19).

Next, we will adjust the Transform tools: *Rotate*, *Scale*, *Shear*, and *Perspective*. Select *Rotate*. With *Show image preview* selected, lower *Image opacity* to *75%* (by clicking on the small down arrow). For *Guides* choose: *No guides* (20).

Do the same for *Scale*, *Shear*, and *Perspective*: set *Image opacity* to *75%*, and set *Guides* to: *No guides*.

Finally, we adjust the *Rectangle* and *Ellipse* select tool. I click on the *Rectangle* select tool.

Now I create a new document by going to: *File > New*, and click on OK.

I drag on the canvas.

Now, below *Fixed*, select the text: Current , and type: 1:1 (so a 1, then a colon, and then a 1 again).

We will do the same for the *Ellipse* select tool. Drag on the canvas. In the *Tool Options* select the text: Current , and type: 1:1.

We are finished configuring the user interface.

Now it's important to *save* the changes we made, so that the next time you open gimp, these settings will be Gimps *default* settings. Go to: *Edit > Preferences*.

In the *Preferences* there are three different places where you save different settings. They are:

1. *Tool Options*
2. *Input Devices*, and
3. *Window Management*.

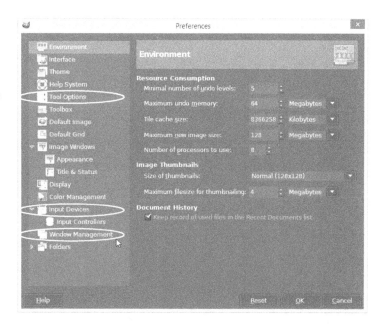

Under *Window Management*, you save which panels are shown, and their position. To save this, click on the: *Save Window Positions Now* button.

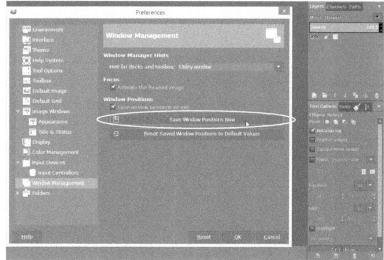

I will also *disable*: *Save window positions on exit*, to prevent that my user interface looks different each time I open Gimp. So I uncheck this option.

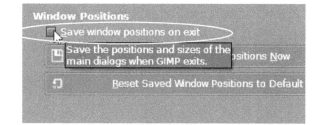

Under *Input Devices*, you save following settings:
a. which *tool* you want to be selected when you start up Gimp
b. which *Fore- and Background colors* you want to have shown by start-up
c. which *brush type* you want to be selected by start-up

The selected tool is by default the *Move* tool, but you could set this for example to the *Brush* tool.
The default *brush* is a *soft* brush, but you can change that to another brush, as we will see later. And you can also change the *Fore- and Background colors* as we will see later.

There is nothing I want to change about these default settings. I like to have the *Move* tool, a *soft* brush, and *black and white* when I open Gimp. If you do change something, then click on the *Save input Device Settings Now* button.

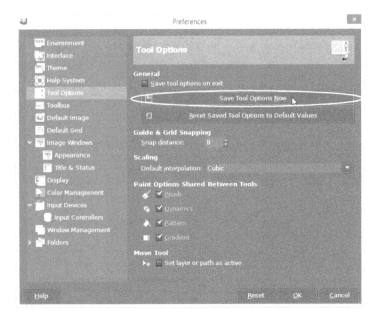

And lastly, under *Tool Options*, we save the changes we have made in the *Tool Options* for the different tools.
To save the changes we made, click on the: *Save Tool Options Now* button.

Click on OK to exit the Preferences.

In the next lesson we will return to the Preferences panel, and adjust some last settings to optimize Gimp.

5. Configuring Preferences

In this lesson, we will dive into Gimp's preferences, and adjust several settings. At the end of this lesson, we're finished optimizing Gimp. Go to: *Edit > Preferences*.

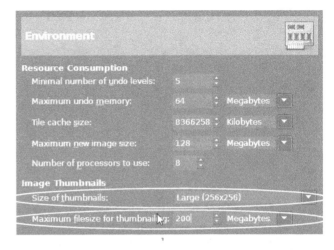

Under *Environment*, Set *Size of thumbnails* to: *Large*. Set *Maximum file size for thumbnailing* to: *200* Megabytes.

Now go to the *User Interface* tab. If you want another language than the one that is shown, you can choose one from the list.

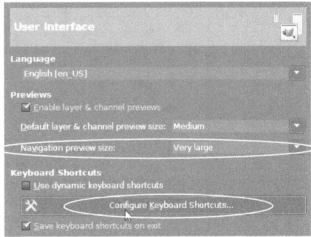

Set *Navigation preview size* (discussed in the Navigation lesson), to: *Very large*.

Now click on the *Configure Keyboard Shortcuts* button.

Open the File folder, by clicking on the small arrow.

Reopening the last opened file, has at the moment the shortcut *Ctrl-1* assigned to it. In Photoshop however, *Ctrl-1* is an important shortcut to make an image visible on screen. Therefore, I will assign a *new* shortcut to this action, so I can use *Ctrl-1* elsewhere.

To assign or change a shortcut, you click on it. You will then see the text appearing:
New accelerator... Then press the new shortcut combination. I choose *Ctrl-Alt-1*.
If *Ctrl-Alt-1* was already used elsewhere, Gimp would tell me that the shortcut is already in use.

Close the *File* folder, and open the *Edit* folder. For deleting the content of a layer, or deleting the content inside a selection, we will assign the *Delete* key to the *Clear* command. I click on *Disabled*, and press the *Delete* key.

Below, when I click on *New Layer* (1), and press: *Ctrl-V*, Gimp notifies me (2) this shortcut is already in use, and asks me if I want to *reassign* the shortcut. This means, that the *original* action will have no shortcut assigned to it anymore.

I want to do this, so I click on *Reassign shortcut*.

We have now placed an existing shortcut on a new location. Pressing *Ctrl-V* will now give me the same behaviour as in Photoshop.

Close the *Edit* folder, and open the *View* folder. Click on *Show Guides* and press: *Ctrl-;* (Ctrl and semicolon). Gimp notifies me this shortcut is already in use. I click on *Reassign shortcut*.

Now go down to where you see twice *1:1 (100%)*. The actions look identical, and they are. I would like to assign *Ctrl-1* to this action, which we made available under *File*.

If your keyboard has *numeric* keys at the right side, your keyboard will have two number 1 keys; one at the top left, and one at the bottom right. I would like to use them both. Click on the top action, the one that has *Ctrl-Alt-0* assigned to it, and press *Ctrl-1*, using the 1 key at the top left side of your keyboard. Then click on the identical action below, which has a *1* assigned to it, and press *Ctrl-1*, now using the *numeric 1* key at the right side of your keyboard.

Next scroll down to *Fit Image in Window*. Here we see *Ctrl-0*. However, the *non-numeric 0* key is used. I will reassign *Ctrl-0*, pressing *Ctrl-0* with the *numeric 0* key, which is easier to use.

Close the *View* folder and open the *Image* folder. Go to *Canvas size*. Click on it and press: *Ctrl-Alt-C*.

On the bottom we have *Scale image*. Click on it and press: *Ctrl-Alt-I*.

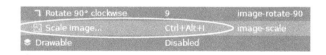

Close the *Image* folder, and open the *Plug-ins* folder. Go to *Save for Web*. Click on it and press: *Shift-Ctrl-Alt-S*.

Now let's use the *Search box* at the top, to find an action. Click in the text entry field and type: `layer`, then a white space, and then the letter `v` (3). Now we get two search results. We're looking for *Layer via Copy*. Click on it and press: *Ctrl-J*. Click on *Reassign shortcut*. To exit Search, clear the Search box.

The last visit is to the *Tools* folder. Scroll down to *Heal*. Click on it and press: *J*. Click on *Reassign shortcut*.

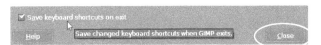

We're finished completing the shortcuts. Click on *Close*. The keyboard shortcuts are saved by default on exit.

Below *Image Windows*, click on *Appearance*.

Here *deselect Show rulers* and *Show layer boundary*, both under *Normal Mode*, and under *Full screen Mode*.

Go to *Display*.
Set *Check Style* to: *Light checks*.

Go to *Color management*.
Set *File open behaviour* to: *Convert to RGB workspace*.

Below *Input Devices* click on *Input Controllers* (4). Here we will add new functionality to the mouse wheel.

At the right, under *Active Controllers*, is the *Main Mouse Wheel*. Double-click on it.

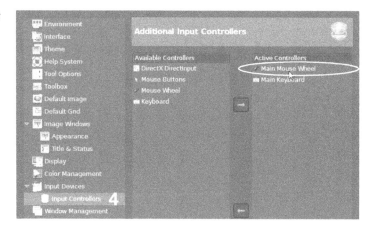

The *Configure Input Controller* window opens.

We will assign new behaviour to scrolling up, and scrolling down, while holding down the *Alt* key. I would like to change the *size* of my brush, by *Alt*-scrolling.

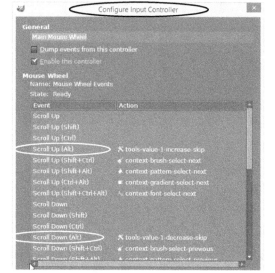

I start with *Scroll Up (Alt)*, and click on it.

Then I click on the *Edit* button.

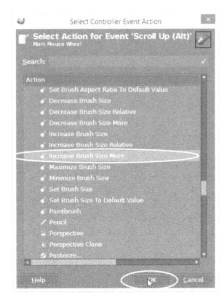

A new window opens. Here I can choose the *new behaviour* for scrolling up while holding *Alt*.

Go to: *Increase Brush Size More*. Click on it,

and click on OK.

Now we will define the behaviour for scrolling down. Click on *Scroll Down (Alt)*,

and click on *Edit*.

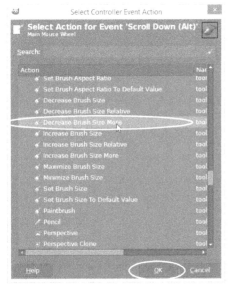

In the new window that opens, click on: *Decrease Brush Size More*,

and click on OK.

We're finished assigning new behaviour for *Alt*-scrolling.
On the bottom right, click on Close.

Finally, we will take a look at how to adjust the Toolbox.

Click on the *Toolbox* tab. Under *Tools configuration* you find all the tools.

When the eye is checked in front of a tool, that tool will be visible in the *toolbox*. To hide a tool, click on the eye, and the tool will disappear from the *toolbox*. The *order* of the tools in the Preferences, is the same as in the Toolbox.

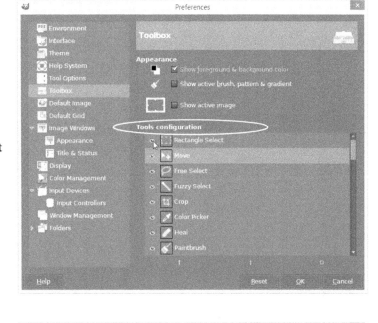

To move a tool to a different location, drag it to another place. You can also use the up and down arrow keys to move a tool. The Toolbox will directly update changes.

You can also work the other way around. When you click on a tool in the Toolbox, this tool will then become the *selected tool* in the Preferences window.

To exit the Preferences click on OK.

We're finished configuring Gimp, let's start learning Gimp!

Chapter 2
Working with layers and color

6. Opening files

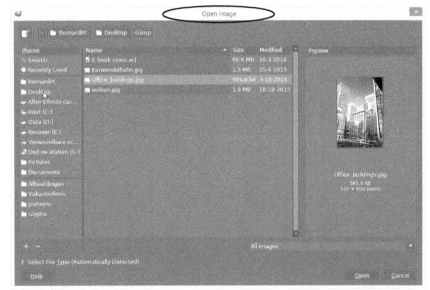

To open an image,
go to *File > Open*.
Notice you can find
it's shortcut, *Ctrl-O*,
at the right side of
the command.
If you click on Open,
the *Open Image*
window opens.

At the left side, under *Places* (1), is the navigation pane.
From here you can access your desktop, your home directory,
the drives on your PC, etc. I will navigate to a folder on my
desktop called *Gimp*. At the left I click on *Desktop*. Then I
double-click on the *Gimp* folder to see its content. At the top
you can see the folders path: *BernardPC > Desktop > Gimp*
(2). To exit the Gimp folder again, and go one step back,
at the top, I can click on the *Desktop* thumbnail, at the left
of the *Gimp* thumbnail (2).

If you visit a specific folder often, you can *bookmark* that
folder for quick access. To bookmark a folder first click on a
folder. Then at the bottom left you will see a blue *plus sign* (3).
When you click on the plus sign, the selected folder is added
to *Places*, at the bottom (4). To remove a bookmarked folder
from the list, click on the bookmark. Then you will see a blue
minus sign (at the right side of the plus sign). Click on the
minus sign to remove the bookmark.

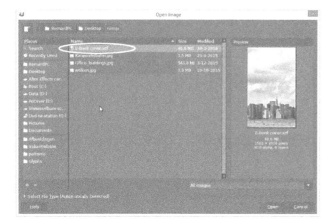

To see a preview of an image you click on the image name. You can also use your up and down arrow keys to browse through a list of images.

By default, the content of a folder is sorted on alphabetical order (*Name*). But you can also sort on date (*Modified*), or sort on file size (*Size*).

To *reverse* a column, to turn it around (for example *file Size*) click on the *Size* thumbnail. Now the list starts with the *smallest* file size, and ends with the *largest* file size (5).

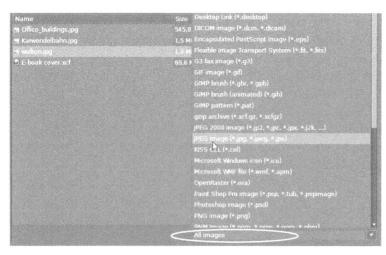

You can also filter the results. Let's say you *only* want to see JPEG images. At the bottom right click on: *All images*, and from the drop down menu choose: *JPEG image*.

Now you will see only the JPEG images that are inside the folder.
I click on *Office_buildings.jpg* and click on Open.

In the next lesson we will look at how to work with layers.

7. Working with layers

As a child, I was fascinated by the way the old Walt Disney cartoons were made. Walt Disney broke down a scene in *moving* and *non-moving* parts. He painted them on different transparent sheets, and laid these transparent sheets on top of each other. Working this way, *only* the sheets with the *changing* elements had to be repainted.

Walt Disney's way of working isn't that different from how we work in Gimp and Photoshop today. Let's open an image with Walt Disney's way of working in mind. Open *Cartoon.xcf*. The images used here come from *Freepik.com*. Open *Layers* by clicking on the *Layers* tab (1). We can see the scene is broken up in three transparent sheets, which in their digital form are now called *layers*.

On the bottom layer is the image of the background. Above the background, we have a layer with only the air balloon on it. And on top we have a layer with only the girl on it.

I have made the layer *thumbnails* a bit larger, so you can better see their content. To do this, click at the right on the *Configure this tab* icon, then go to *Preview Size*, and choose *Gigantic* (2). Now you can clearly see what is on the three layers. If you hold your mouse pressed down on a layer thumbnail, you get an even bigger preview of its content, as we can see with the air balloon (3).

You can move the layers *independent* of each other. To move the girl layer, select the layer where the girl is on, by clicking on that layer. Also select the *Move* tool. The *Move* tool can be found in the toolbar at the left (4). You can click on it, or press the letter *V* to select it. Now you can move the girl around by dragging on the canvas (5).

If you press *Ctrl-Z*, which can be found under: *Edit > Undo*, you undo your move, and the girl is back where you started. And if you want to move the air balloon, click on the air balloon layer, and move the air balloon.

With the air balloon layer selected, you can't move the girl. However, if you click in the *Tool Options* on: *Pick a layer or guide* (6), it will become possible. If you now place your mouse *above* the girl, you will see a *hand* appearing at the right side of the cursor (7). Even though the girl layer is *not* the selected layer, you *are* able to move her now. After moving the girl layer, the balloon layer will *still* be the selected layer, so that hasn't changed (8).

This way of moving we just did, *isn't* set as the default in Gimp, and also isn't the default in Photoshop. The reason for this is the possibility of moving other layers *by accident*, without noticing. However, when you quickly have to move several different layers, it's possible to do this quickly by selecting the *Pick a layer* option. I will select the *Move the active layer* option again.

It's also possible to move more than one layer at the same time. Let's say you want to drag the girl layer *together* with the air balloon layer. To do this you can temporarily *link* these layers. If you click between the eye and the thumbnail, a *chain icon* appears (9). Layers that have a chain, are linked to each other. If you move a layer that has a chain, other layers that also have a chain, will move with it. To remove a chain, click on the chain again.

The *checkerboard* pattern is a visual way to show empty space. It's like the transparent sheet from the old days; where there was no paint, you could look *through* it. Our background is completely filled. However, if we move the background to the side, we also get to see the checkerboard pattern.

To change the *stacking order* of a layer, simply drag the layer up or down. Right now, the girl is *in front* of the air balloon (10). If I want to place her *behind* the air balloon, I drag the girl layer down.

When you see an extra arrow and a white line appearing (11), release the mouse. The girl is now behind the air balloon (12, 13).

You can also click on the up and down *arrows* to move a layer up or down (14). I will put her back on top.

You can hide a layer by clicking on the eye at the left of the layer thumbnail. Click there again, and the layer is visible again. If you *Shift*-click on a layers eye, you will *solo* that layer. This means you will see *only* that layer, and hide all other layers (15). *Shift*-click on the eye again, and all layers are visible again.

You can also lower a layer's *Opacity*. Lowering a layer's Opacity means you make the content on that layer more *transparent*. This means you can then look *through* the content.

Select the girl layer. Place your cursor in the opacity bar, close to the top edge (16). You will see an arrow that points upwards. If you drag to the left, you will slowly see the girl disappear (17, 18).

Moving your cursor to the bottom edge, will make the arrow change to a *double-sided* arrow (19). The double-sided arrow can be used for fine-tuning. And when your cursor is *inside* the Opacity bar, you can also use your *scroll wheel* to adjust the opacity.

When you know the exact percentage you want, you can directly *type* it, by *triple*-clicking on the text at the right, type a number, and press Enter.

If you want to *delete* a layer you click on it, and at the bottom right click on the *trash can*. You can undo this by pressing *Ctrl-Z*.

You can make a *duplicate* of a layer by clicking on the *Create a duplicate* button (20). Let's duplicate the girl. Now we have two layers with the girl on it. I drag it to the side (21). I delete the duplicate again.

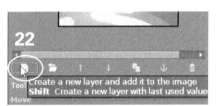

You can create a *new* and empty layer, by holding the *Shift* key down, and then click on the *Create a new layer* button (22). If you get a layer that is not empty, click on the *Create a new layer* button without the Shift key, choose: *Transparency* (23), and click on OK. From now on when you *Shift*-click on the *Create a new layer* button, you will get an empty layer.

You can give a layer a *name*. The more layers you get, the more helpful this will be for quickly recognising what's on a layer. You can double-click on a layers *thumbnail*, type a name (24), and press Enter. You can also double-click on the *text itself* at the right side of the layers thumbnail, type a name, and press Enter.

I have set the layer thumbnails to *medium* size again, and copied the girl layer several times to get more layers than the panel can show. I am now *still* able to *drag* a layer to another place. If I drag a layer from the top completely to the bottom, the panel will *auto scroll* (see the change of the scroll bar, between the left and right image).

The fastest way to place a layer on *top* or on the *bottom*, is to *Shift*-click on the pointing *up* arrow to place the layer at the top (25, 26), or *Shift*-click on the pointing *down* arrow to place the layer at the bottom.

In the next lesson we will look at a special layer: the Background.

8. The 'background' layer

Gimp and Photoshop have a lot in common. One of these things is the mystery of the Background layer. So, what is the Background layer? If you create a *new* document, or you open for example a *jpeg* image in Gimp or Photoshop, you will start with a special layer: the *Background*. In Photoshop you can recognize the Background because it has *italic* text instead of normal text. In Gimp you can recognize the Background because it has *bold* text instead of normal text.

The Background is different from a normal layer, because you can't look through it. We can see this in the Layers panel. At the left we see the *same* layer twice. However, the bottom layer is a *Background* layer. As we can see, there is no checkerboard pattern there. Instead we see black pixels. The black pixels visualise that the layer doesn't have transparency (for example for use on the internet, see p. 112). So how do we change this?

In both Photoshop and Gimp you can *right*-click on the Background. In Photoshop you choose: *Layer from background* (1). In Gimp, you choose: *Add Alpha Channel* (2). Both do the same.

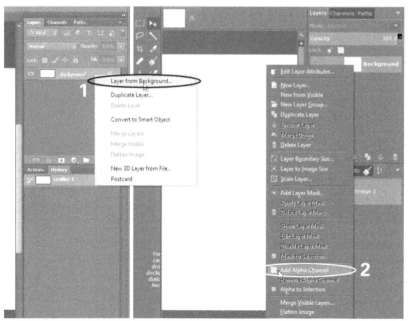

In Gimp, the bold text will now change to normal text. The Background has become a *normal* layer.

In the next lecture we will look at how to navigate in Gimp.

9. Zooming and panning

For this lesson, open *Mountains.jpg*. There are two main ways of navigation: zooming and panning. Let's start with zooming.
Zooming means zooming in and zooming out. The fastest way to zoom is by scrolling with the mouse wheel while holding down the *Ctrl* key. If you scroll forward, you zoom *in*, if you scroll backward, you zoom *out*. The place you hold your mouse, is the place you will zoom in on. This is very efficient. Let's say I want to zoom in on a screw. I hold my cursor above it (1), press *Ctrl*, and scroll forward (2). If you zoom in very far, you will start to see the building blocks of the image, the *pixels*.

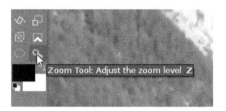

Another way to zoom is using the *Zoom* tool. It's located at the bottom of the toolbar. With the Zoom tool you can drag an *exact area* you want to zoom in on (3).

The fastest way to zoom out again is by pressing: *Ctrl-0*. *Ctrl-0* will *fit* the image perfectly on the screen. Although fitting an image on the available space on screen is very useful, it *doesn't* mean that you then see the image at its *real* size. To see an image at it's *real* size, it's zoom percentage has to be: 100%. Anything *higher* than 100% means you're zoomed in, anything *lower* than 100% means you're zoomed out.

The zoom percentage is shown at the bottom of the screen. We see: *19,5 %* (4). This means we're zoomed *out*. The image is *much larger*, than what we see right now.

When you see an image at it's *real* size, so at 100%, *each* pixel of the *image*, will correspond to a pixel of your *screen* (so an *exact* match). The shortcut for real size, or 100%, is: *Ctrl-1*.

The second way of navigating is panning. When you're zoomed *in* on an image, you can move around, or pan, by pressing down your *scroll* wheel, and then move your mouse.

You can also just scroll with your mouse wheel to move up and down. And when you add the *Shift* key while scrolling, you will move to the left and the right.

For moving over *longer distances*, dragging the scroll bar at the right (5) and at the bottom works fast and efficient.

Finally, at the bottom right of the canvas there is the *Navigate display* (6). When you click on the *little cross*, a thumbnail of the image appears (7).

In the *Navigate display* you can move around by dragging inside the *white border*. The white border represents the visual canvas.

In the next lesson we will explore the paintbrush.

10. Using the paintbrush

Now let's look at the paintbrush. Open *Paragliders.jpg*. Before using the paintbrush, I will create a new empty layer, so I am not painting on the image, but on a separate layer (and so leave the image in tact).

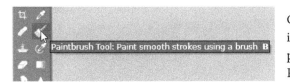

Click on the *Paintbrush* tool in the toolbar. You can also press: *B* to select the Paintbrush.

To change the *size* of the brush, press the *Alt* key, and scroll forward to increase the size (1), and scroll backward to decrease the size (2).
In the *Tool Options*, you can see the size of the brush changing. I set the size to 60. The color you'll will be painting with comes from the *Foreground* color, which is by default set to black (3). Behind the Foreground color is the *Background* color (4), which is by default set to white. You can turn them around by clicking on the little double arrow, or by pressing the *X* key.

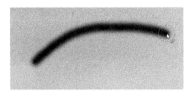

To draw a stroke you drag.

To draw a straight line, click once (5), then press *Shift*, and with Shift pressed down, click somewhere else (6).

To get a straight *horizontal* or *vertical* line, press *Shift* plus *Control*. The thin line (7) is a *preview* to help you see where the stroke will be.

In the *Tool Options*, you can see a small thumbnail (8). This is the brush you're currently using. If you click on it (9), you will get an overview of all the brushes you have. I have added some additional brushes. At the end of this lesson, I will show you where you can download *free* creative brushes.

Another way to select a brush is by going to the *Brushes* panel (10). I open it. The advantage of the *Brushes* panel is that you can make the panel larger, by dragging at the side.

As in the *Layers* panel, you can also make the *thumbnails* of the brushes bigger in the *Brushes* panel. I click on *Configure this tab*, go to *Preview size*, and I select *Extra large*.

A small *plus* sign at the bottom right of a brush icon means that the *actual* brush size is *larger* than the preview size. As in the layers panel, you get a *larger* preview if you click on the thumbnail and hold the mouse button down (11).

A brush with a *red triangle* is called an *animated* brush. An animated brush will alternate different brushes while you paint, so it gives variation in the paint result.

A brush with a *blue triangle* is created inside Gimp's own *Brush Editor*. Let's have a look at the Brush Editor.
If you double-click on a brush with a blue triangle, the *Brush Editor* opens. Here you can see the *settings* that the brush has (12).
Because Gimp's own brushes are locked, you *can't change* the brush. So we will make some brushes of our own, that we can tweak when needed.

To make a new brush, at the bottom of the Brushes panel, click on the *Create a new brush* button.

I go to the *Brush Editor*. I increase *Radius* a bit to get a larger preview. Below the preview, you can choose between three basic shapes: *Circle*, *Square*, and *Diamond*. Click on the *Diamond* shape icon (13). In the *Spikes* bar, by scrolling with your scroll wheel, make about 10 spikes (14). If you now increase the *Aspect ratio* (15), you'll create a star (16). If you click on the *Circle* icon, you will get rounded corners (17), resulting in a flower shape. And if you click on the *Square*, you will get straight lines (18).

Select the *Diamond* again. Lowering the *Hardness* (19) makes the brush softer (20). Let's test the brush. I will paint with white.

I increase the size of my brush by *Alt*-scrolling it to about 300. The brush gives a sun effect (21).

I choose *Circle* again, remove *Spikes* (22), and set *Hardness* to 100%. You can flatten the brush with *Aspect ratio* (23), and rotate it with *Angle* (24).

Notice that *Aspect ratio* (25) and *Angle* (26) can also be adjusted in the *Tool Options* (with finished brushes). The changes made in the *Tool Options* however are only *temporarily*, and will not be saved. The three icons at the right are *reset* buttons to set the brushes back to their default values.

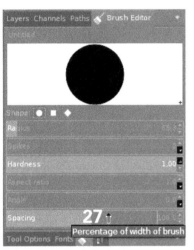

Spacing (27) determines how often the brush repeats itself when you draw. With a Spacing of 100%, the brush will repeat itself after its *own length*.

A fast way to *clear* the *content* of the layer you're painting on is by pressing the *Delete* key. If you now draw with a circle, the circles will touch each other (28). To reach *fluid* lines, you will need a Spacing of *10%*.

Spacing (like *Aspect ratio* and *Angle*) is *also* adjustable at a later point. At the bottom of the *Brushes panel*, you can adjust the *Spacing* of a finished brush (29). Changes to *Spacing* in the *Brushes panel* will (like changes to *Aspect ratio* and *Angle* in the *Tool Options*) not be saved.

In the Brushes panel you can also *delete* a brush. I click on the brush we just made (30). A selected brush has a black border around it. At the bottom I click on the *Delete this brush* (trash can) icon. Then I click on Delete (31).

Now we quickly make our own set of soft round brushes. Click on the *Create a new brush* button at the bottom of the *Brushes panel*.

We start by giving the brush a name. On the top, select the text *Untitled*. Type: `Brush`, and then press the space bar once to put an extra white space behind the text. Press *Ctrl-A* and *Ctrl-C* to copy the text, so we can use the text again for the other brushes. Now click behind the text, so you see a blinking cursor again,

and add the text: `25% (32)`.

Next, hold your mouse above the *Hardness* bar (33), and scroll backwards to *25%* (indicated at the right as: *0,25*). Press the *Tab* key three times to get the text *highlighted* at *Spacing* (34), and type: `10` (to set the *Spacing* to 10). The first brush is ready.

Click again on the *Create a new brush* button. Double-click at the top on the text *Untitled*, and press *Ctrl-V* to paste the copied text. Type: `90%`. Click once in the *Hardness* bar around *90%*, then scroll with your scroll wheel to *90%*. Press *Tab* three times, and type: `10`. The second brush is ready.
Click again on the *Create a new brush* button. Double-click on the text *Untitled* and press *Ctrl-V*. Type: `0%`. Drag *Hardness* all the way to the left, to *0%*. Press *Tab* three times, and type: `10`. The third brush is ready.
Click again on the *Create a new brush* button. Select *Untitled* and press *Ctrl-V*. Type: `100%`. Drag the *Hardness* all the way to the right, to *100%*. Press *Tab* three times, and type: `10`. The brushes are finished!

In the *Brushes* panel we can see the four brushes we made. I would like to set *one* of these brushes as the *default* brush. This means that every time I start up Gimp, and I select the Paintbrush, this brush will be the brush that's selected in the *Tool Options*. I select *Brush 0%* (I will see a black border around it). At the top of the window I can see it's name (and dimensions).

Now I go to *Edit > Preferences > Input Devices*. As mentioned in lesson 4, under *Input Devices* you specify: 1) the *default tool*, 2) the *Fore- and Background color*, and 3) the *brush type*.

I have selected a new brush (Brush 0%) to be the *default* brush. *Before* I save my new brush choice, I make sure the *Move* tool is selected, and the *Fore- and Background* colors are set to their default *black and white*. When they are not, you can click on the *small* black and white icon at the bottom left (35), or press: *D*.

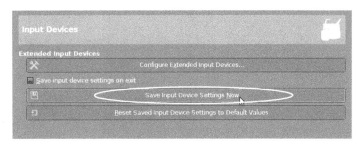

Now I save my selected brush as the default brush. I click on: *Save Input Device Settings now.*

In the next lesson we will look at how to create special effects with the brush.

11. Brush special effects

Select a soft brush and set the brush size to 40. If you click on the *icon* at the left of *Dynamics* (1), you will see a list with options.

Select: *Velocity Tapering*. What *Velocity Tapering* does is, it decreases the *size* ánd *opacity* of your brush, when you move your mouse *faster* (2).

Below *Dynamics*, there is an option *Apply Jitter* (3). *Jitter* will spread the brush randomly (4). When you select *Apply Jitter*, you can set the *Amount*. Increasing *Amount* will lead to a *larger area* in which the spreading will take place. I set Jitter to about 4 by dragging at the bottom of the Amount bar (5).

Click on the icon at the left of *Dynamics* again, and now select: *Speed Size Opacity*.

To demonstrate this Dynamic, I will use a brush I have downloaded, named *Birdsflying_11*. At the end of this lesson I will show you where to download free brushes.

I will search for: *Birdsflying_11*. To search a brush *by name*, in the *Tool Options*, click on the brush thumbnail (6), and then select *View as list* at the bottom. To go through the list fast you can drag the scroll bar at the right (7). When you're close to the destination, you can further scroll with your scroll wheel. I select *Birdsflying_11*.

I choose black to paint black birds. I *Alt*-scroll to set the brush size to 150, and I will increase *Jitter* to about 15.

We can see that *Speed Size Opacity* follows the *direction* of the *mouse* (8, 9 10).

It also *decreases* the size of the brush when you move the mouse faster.

The next dynamic I would like to show you is *Dynamics random*.

I will choose another downloaded brush, named *bubble_brushes_by _hawksmont3*.

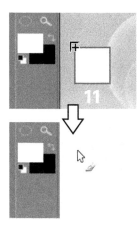

I will set the size to 250, and press *X* to paint with white.

To show the next brush I will make a white layer. I create an empty layer by *Shift*-clicking on the *Create a new layer* button. To fill the layer with white, I *drag* the Foreground color, which is white now, *on* the canvas (11). This way of filling is *Gimp only*. You can't do this in Photoshop. The Photoshop way of filling can be found under: *Edit > Fill with FG color*. The shortcut for this is *Alt-Backspace*.

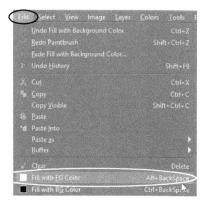

Now press *X* to set the Foreground color to black. We will make a grungy effect. In the *Tool Options* I select a Gimp brush called: *Acrylic 05*. The default Gimp brushes are at the bottom. I set the brush size to 400, and disable *Jitter*.

When I now set *Dynamics* on *Perspective*, I can make grungy strokes.

I set the brush to a 100% hard brush, size 80. I set *Dynamics* on *Pen Generic*. *Pen Generic* simulates writing with ink. I write the Dutch greeting *hallo*.

To draw with chalk, I select *Texture Hose 01*. I now choose: *Dynamics Off*, which means *no* dynamics are applied. I set the brush size to 20.

With *Fade Tapering* the brush fades in or out. Right now it fades in.

When you open *Dynamics Options* (12), you can *reverse* the fading direction by clicking on *Reverse* (13). I increase the Fade length a bit to 400.

Now the brush fades out.

Each time you start up Gimp, *Pressure Opacity* is the default brush Dynamic. For the mouse, *Pressure Opacity* has no effect. But if you are using a tablet, it enables you to draw with *pressure sensitivity*.

In the next lesson we will look at using a tablet.

12. Using a tablet

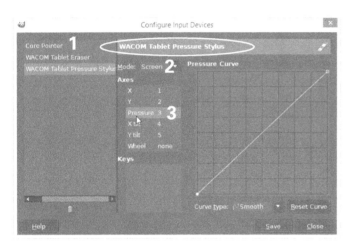

We start by looking at the tablet preferences. Go to: *Edit > Preferences > Input Devices > Configure Extended Input Devices.* I have connected a *Wacom Tablet Pressure Stylus* as we can see at the top. The *Core Pointer* (1) is my mouse. Below we see: *WACOM Tablet Eraser*, which is the bottom of my pen, with which I can erase. The *Wacom Tablet Pressure Stylus* is the top of my pen, with which I can draw. Both are set on *Screen* (2).

When I click on *Pressure* (3), I can change the *sensitivity* of the tablet. The horizontal axis, is pen *pressure*, starting with low pen pressure to higher pen pressure. The vertical axis is the *brush visibility*, starting from not visible, to fully visible. So the harder I press my pen, the darker or more visible the brush will become.

Let's say I want to press *less hard* before I start to see my brush. I can adjust this by dragging the *left side* of the graph up (4). And if I want to press less hard before I reach the *maximum* brush visibility, I drag the *right side* of the graph to the *left* (5).

For fine-tuning, I would like that pressing just a bit harder doesn't lead to high brush visibility so fast. To do this, I will flatten the graph at the beginning a bit by dragging it down (6). You will see an *extra point* is automatically created to make this possible.

Now I save the tablet settings. We are under *Input Devices*, where also the default *Tool, Fore- and Background color*, and *brush type* are saved. So before I click on Save, I make sure that they are set correctly (the *Move* tool, *black and white*, and a *soft brush*). Then I click on *Save*, and on Close.
To close the Preferences, I click on OK.

If the *back* of the pen *doesn't* erase, you can do the following: select the *Erase Tool* (7) with the *back* of the pen, and then *use* the back of the pen (8). Switching between *pen* (front) and *eraser* (back) will work now.

To download *free* brushes, you can do a Google search for: *gimp free brushes*. There are several websites you can go to. I downloaded my brushes from *deviantart.com*. Click on the Browse tab, and in the Search box type: *gimp brushes*. If you scroll to the bottom you can click on *Show more*. If you find a brush-pack you like, you can click on it.

At the right, you will see a download button. After downloading, Unzip the file.

A *.gbr* extension stands for: *gimp brush*, and a *.gih* extension stands for: *gimp animated brush*. Go to the *.gimp-2.8 folder* where you've placed the plugins, and open the *brushes* folder. Place the downloaded brushes in this folder. In Gimp, I go to the *Brushes* panel, and click at the bottom right on the *Refresh brushes* icon (9). The new brushes are now ready to use.

In the next lecture we will look at how to go back in time with the History panel.

13. The history panel

For undoing multiple steps, in Gimp and Photoshop you have the *History* panel. To see how the *History* panel works, we'll create a new document. Go to: *File > New*. Make *Width* and *Height* 500 pixels.

If you open *Advanced Options*, you will see *Fill with* is by default the *Background color*. This means the new document will be filled with white. Click on OK.

Open the *History* panel at the bottom right. In the *History* panel we see a *Base Image* thumbnail. Select the *Brush* tool, and in the *Tool Options* select a hard brush. Set the size to 150. Open the *History* panel again.

When I click with my brush at the top left of my document to add a point, a new state is added to the *History* panel (1). The thumbnail visually shows us a point is added, and in the description we can read that we used the *paintbrush* to do this. Let's click three more times. I can now see I have used the *paintbrush* four times (2).

Let's say at this point I realize I made a mistake. I wanted 3 dots *diagonally*.

To go back in time, I can click on a previous state. I can also use my up- and down *arrow* keys, to 'walk' through my history. Nothing will be deleted when you navigate through your history.

I would like to go back to the situation where I had just *one* point. I want this state to be my new starting point. When I start working from this point, a new state will be added again, but all the *future* states will be *deleted*. This deleting cannot be undone. If you want to prevent this deleting, continue working in a *duplicate* of your file. Go to: *Image > Duplicate*, to duplicate your file. The *duplicated* image has the state that was *selected* in your *original* file in the *History* panel, when you made the duplicate. You can now continue working in the *duplicated* file, while in the *original* image all the future states are still intact! At the moment you are sure that you *don't* need these future states anymore, you can delete the original file.

The number of steps you can go back in time is not infinite, however normally sufficient. If you're not satisfied with the amount of steps you can go back, you can go to: *Edit > Preferences*, or press *Ctrl-K*. The absolute minimum number of undo levels is now set to 5. This means Gimp guarantees, that you can go *at least* 5 steps back, at any time (3). The actual number of steps you can go back is normally much higher, dependent of how *large* your file is, and how *memory intensive* your changes were.

Maximum undo memory (4) is for computers that don't have much RAM. If a computer hasn't much RAM, lowering the amount of allocated RAM for Maximum undo memory, *together* with lowering the *Minimal number of undo levels*, can help increasing overall performance. For computers that have a sufficient amount of RAM, *Maximum undo memory* does not have to be adjusted.

In the next lesson we will look at color.

14. HSV color

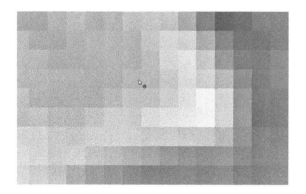

Image manipulation programs are all about color. How to select color, and how to change color. If we zoom in closely on an image, we see that an image consists of *squares*, with each square having its own color. These squares are called *pixels*, and a digital camera captures millions of them in a photo. One million pixels is often referred to as a megapixel.

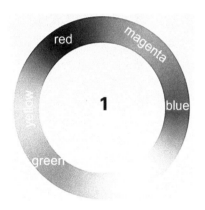

To get a better understanding of how you can manipulate color, we'll look in this lesson at the *three core components* that define color. They are described in the *HSV color model*, which is short for: *Hue, Saturation*, and *Value*. In Gimp and Photoshop you can adjust each of these color components *separately*, which is really powerful.

The first component of HSV is *Hue*, which can be *any color* on the Hue ring (1).
The second component is *Saturation*. The colors on the Hue ring are *fully* saturated.

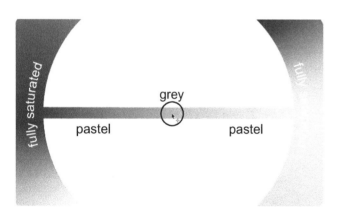

If we *connect* the colors from one side of the ring, to the opposite side of the ring, we will see that in the *middle* we find pure *grey*, which means colors in the middle have become fully *unsaturated*. So at the *edge* all colors are fully saturated, and in the *center* all colors have become fully *unsaturated*. When a color is going from fully saturated more to grey, we call it *pastel* colors. So colors in the center are fully unsaturated, than they go to *pastels*, and at the outside the colors are fully saturated.

The third and last component is *Value*. Value determines how *dark* or how *light* a color is. Bringing the Value down, which is the same as bringing in *black*, leads to darker, *shadowy* colors. Bringing the Value up, which is the same as bringing in *white*, makes the colors *lighter*. When colors become white, they are said to be *fully illuminated* (2).

To represent Hue, Saturation, and Value *all three together*, we would get a *cylindrical* model.

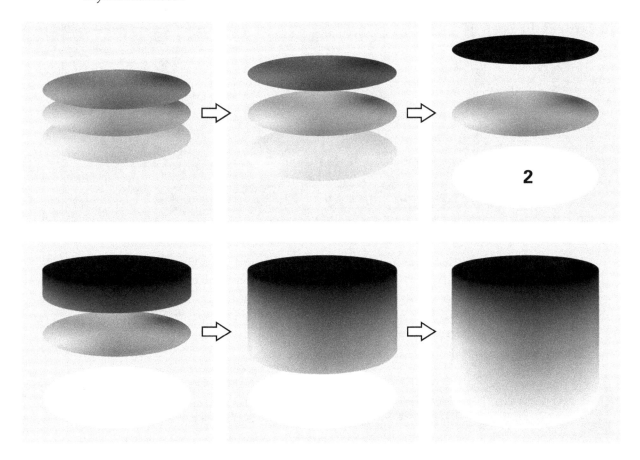

In the next lecture we will look at the RGB color model.

15. RGB color

In the previous lecture we have looked at Hue, Saturation, and Value, as described in the *HSV color model*. In this lecture we will look at the *RGB color model*. RGB stands for *Red*, *Green*, and *Blue*. It is the color model that a digital camera uses, as well as your computer screen. An image from a digital camera is actually built up from three images: a *red*, a *green*, and a *blue* image (1, 2, 3).

This means that *each pixel* of an image has information about how much red, green, and blue it contains. If we compare the red, green, and blue images, we can see that the sky in the *red* image is very dark (1). The sky in the *green* image is lighter (2), and the sky in the *blue* image is the lightest. We will see what this means in a moment.

Click on Foreground color, to open the *Change Foreground Color* window. At the top we have a *Hue*, *Saturation*, and *Value* slider (from the *HSV color model*). And under it, we have a *Red*, *Green*, and *Blue* slider, with which we can create any color in the *RGB color model*. So two color models are shown here *together*, and they also can be *used* together! Right now we have the color black (the Foreground color is black), which means: *red*, *green*, and *blue* all have a value of 0 (4). So the description for black in *RGB* is: (0,0,0). With the sliders we can change this.

Let's adjust the *red*, *green*, and *blue* values, and see what happens. I start by dragging the Red slider all the way to the right (5). We now get *full* red, and red has become a value of *255*. The number 255 isn't a coincidence. The tiny red, green, and blue lights that make up your computer screen, are also dimmable in 255 steps, from fully *off* to fully *on*.

Now let's also drag the Green slider all the way to the right. The result is that we see yellow! The color yellow is somewhat counterintuitive, because we are *used* to mixing paint on paper, and mixing red and green *doesn't* make yellow.

The answer lies in the terms *additive*, versus *subtractive* color. RGB is an *additive* color system. In this image we can see how it works. The image represents a fully *unilluminated* white wall, which is illuminated by three *colored* flashlights; a *red*, a *green*, and a *blue* flashlight. Where two flashlights *overlap*, the color changes, and the wall gets *brightened up* even more. In the middle, where the *red*, *green*, and *blue* flashlights *all* overlap, we are now able to see the wall as it is; in *white*! This is how the RGB color model works. The white wall is made visible by *adding* colored lights, hence the name

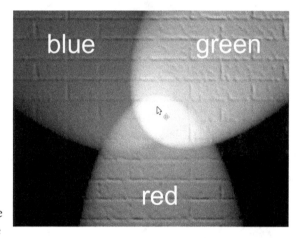

additive color. When we print an image, all the paint will do, is make the already white and illuminated paper *darker*, hence the name *subtractive* color. So additive and subtractive color work in *opposite* ways.

Where the red and green flashlights overlap, we get yellow.

A digital camera works with the RGB color model. This means a digital camera will capture *three* images; a red, a green, and a blue image. Gimp and Photoshop will *show* us these three images, in the panel at the right side of Layers, called *Channels*. So the red, green, and blue images are called *channels*.
Gimp shows each channels on the canvas in *color* for us, but the channels are actually just *black and white* images (as is shown in the thumbnails).

As you can hide layers, you can also hide channels. So hiding the Green channel, will turn the green flashlight off.

When we look at the channels of a Hue ring (a ring with all colors), we can see *all* Hue's are created with only three basic colors. How is this possible?

The reason for this is that our eyes can *also* perceive *only* red, green, and blue information. Our brain does the rest; it will mix these three basic colors, and we see *all* colors.

To create a certain color in the *Change Foreground Color* window, you can also drag your mouse in the *color square* at the left. Here we see a *horizontal* line (6), and a *vertical* line (7).

The horizontal line is the *Saturation* of a color. Dragging *down* will desaturate the color, dragging *up* will increase the saturation of the color.

The vertical line is the *Value* of a color. Moving to the left makes the color *darker*, moving to the right makes the color *lighter*.

The *Hue* of a color can be chosen at the right side of the square (8); in the *hue strip*. The *hue strip* is a *straightened* Hue ring. You can slide through the hues by dragging (9).

When you found a color, and you close the window by clicking OK, the *new* color will be added to the *Color history*. The *Color history* are the 12 color icons below the *HTML notation* (10).

You can also add colors to the color history by clicking on the arrow button at the left of the color history. When a new color is added, all colors shift one place to the right, and the oldest swatch (at the bottom right) will be deleted. If you need the HTML, or *hexadecimal* notation of a color for the internet, you can copy it's value from above the color history.

In the next lecture we will look at how to make an image darker or lighter (*Value*), with Levels.

16. Levels

In the *HSV color model*, we saw the three basic elements of color are: *Hue*, *Saturation*, and *Value*. Levels is a powerful tool to adjust *Value*. So with Levels you can change how dark or light an image is.

Open *Amsterdam.jpg*. Here we have an image of Amsterdam, taken with a bright sky in the background. To protect the image from overexposure, the camera closed its lens a bit. As a result of this, the darker areas in the image didn't get enough light. Fortunately, in an image manipulation program it's easy to correct for underexposure.

Open Levels by going to: *Colors > Levels*, or press *Ctrl-L*. In the window there are five sliders. For *most* corrections, however, you will be using only *one*; the *middle* slider at the top (1). This slider is very powerful. With this slider you're able to make your image darker or lighter, *without* losing the darkest or lightest colors. This means the *Value* of all colors are intelligently *stretched*.

If you drag the middle slider to the left, the image brightens up (2). And if you drag it to the right, the image darkens (3). I want to brighten the image up.

So what do the two black sliders and the two white sliders do? The top black slider makes dark colors darker, and the top white slider makes light colors lighter. So when is this neccessary?

Let's have a look at how the program can help us with that question. Open *Mountains.jpg*, and open Levels again.

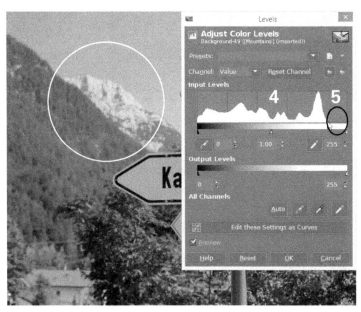

The graph we see here is called a *histogram*. The *histogram* shows us how *many* dark pixels there are in the image, up until how *many* light pixels there are in the image. Our histogram shows that this image *doesn't* have colors in the *brightest* area (5).

So what can we do with this information? If we want to introduce more *bright* colors in the image (and we do, to get the snow really white), we can drag the white slider to the point where the histogram *ends* (6).

Now we let our eyes decide if this improves our image. On the bottom left you have a *Preview* button (7). By clicking on it, you can compare the before and after. I think this improves the image. The snow on the mountain has become white (isn't greyish anymore).

Now what about the black slider? As we can see in the histogram, the image doesn't mis any dark colors (there are colors up until the deepest blacks). So what would happen if we drag the black slider to the right, *inside* the colors of the histogram? What then happens is called **clipping**. All the darkest colors inside your image, that find themselves at the *left* side of the *black* slider, will now become *completely black* (8). Their *Hue* will become 0. So *clipping* means *losing* visual information in either the shadows or highlights, although it may not always be that noticeable. So *Value* adjustments with the top *black* and top *white* slider can sometimes be a trade-off between getting a desired overall *Value* effect, and having some clipping. Most of the time however, dragging the black and white slider to the point where the graph ends (as we did with the white slider to get the snow white), is enough to get an *optimal* and *balanced* result. Thereby, a *solútion* for clipping can be using *Curves*, which we will look at in the next lesson.

The bottom black and white sliders work in the opposite way as the top black and white sliders. Where the top black slider makes dark colors *darker*, the bottom black slider makes dark colors *lighter*. This will make the image look a bit washed out.

And where the top white slider makes light colors *lighter*, the bottom white slider makes light colors *darker*.
For correcting *Value*, the bottom black and white slider are seldom used.

You can also use Levels to change color, so; *Hue*. Open *Color_cast.xcf*. Here we have an image with a reddish color cast (the image looks red). Why is this? If you open the *Channels* panel, and look at the channels, you can see the Red channel is much *lighter* than the other two channels. This means there is much more red, than green and blue in the image. If we think back of the flashlights and the *unilluminated* wall, here the battery of the red *flashlight* (which is the red *channel*) is ok, but the green and blue flashlights don't give as much light (like their batteries are almost empty). As a result, the red flashlight *predominates*, which imbalances the color of the image.

We will now look at *three ways* to get the three channels at an equal level (to get all batteries *fully* charged).

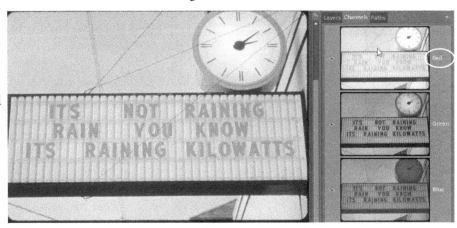

For the *first* method, I will *darken* the red channel, to get the brightness of the three channels equal, which will remove the color cast. When the color cast is gone, I will brighten up *all three* channels at the same time, so, equally. Let's have a look.

Open *Levels*. If we look behind *Channel*, we see we are by default adjusting the *Value* (9). This *actually* means, we're adjusting the Value of *all three color channels* at the *same time* (so for red, green, and blue equally). You can however also adjust a *single* color channel *separately*.

If you click on *Value*, you can see the *Red*, *Green* and *Blue* channels (10). Changing the Value for a *single* color channel, will change the color, or *Hue*, of the image!

Because the *Red* channel is lighter than the other two channels, we will first *darken* the *Red* channel, in order to remove the color cast.

Choose the *Red* channel. To darken the Red channel, drag the middle slider to the *right*, until the image doesn't look red anymore. The image as a *whole*, has become darker now. To adjust this, go back to *Value* (to adjust the Value of the *three color channels at the same time*) and brighten the image up, by dragging the middle slider this time to the *left*.

For the *second* method, we will look at the *histograms* of each channel *separately*. To go back to the *original* red image, you can use the *History* panel, or you can go to: *File > Revert* (this brings the image back to how it was when you opened it).

Open Levels. When you hold your mouse *above* Value, you can *scroll* with your mouse to look at the individual histograms of the three channels. We can see that the *Green* and *Blue* channel, are missing a lot of *highlights*.

I could manually optimize each channel (by dragging the *black* and *white* sliders to *fit* the *histograms*), but Gimp will do this *for* me. When you click on the *Auto* button (10), all three histograms are *optimized*.

We see that by pressing a *single* button, we're able to remove almost *all* of the color cast.

For the *third method*, we will use the three *Value pickers* at the right side of the *Auto* button. They are the **black point** (11), the **grey point** (12), and the **white point** (13) picker.

You can use just one, two, or all three of them. Let's start with the *white point picker* at the right. I select it. The place where I *click* on in the image, will become completely white (like the top *white slider* of the *histogram*, is placed at *that* Value point). I can *click* in the sky, by I can also *drag* in the sky, to quickly see different results.

Making the *sky white*, results in a somewhat *yellowish* image. This probably means that the sky *wasn't neutral white* when this picture was made, but probably had some *blue* in it.

So let's try another light point, for example on a light point on the sign (14). The result now looks good.

Let's move on to the *grey point picker*. Finding a grey point can be difficult because we're not sure what area in the image was originally *neutral grey*. So I will experiment again. Although it is a bit dark,

clicking at the center of the hands of the clock (15) seems to neutralise the color cast *even more*, so I will use this area.

And lastly, I select the *black point picker*. For the black point picker, I will look for a very *dark shadow area*, like the *bottom* of the sign board (16). The result looks good now.

In the next lesson we will meet Levels big brother: Curves.

17. Curves

In many cases, Levels will give you the result you're looking for. However, if you need more control, *Curves* will give you that. Open *Amsterdam.jpg* again. Go to: *Colors > Curves*.
In Curves, you can *create* as many 'sliders' as you want, *yourself*.
By *default*, you have a black (1) and a white (2) *point*, which are the little circles at the bottom and the top of the line. Now we are going to *add* a point ourselves (3), to recreate the *midpoint* slider we have in *Levels*.

To add a point, just click somewhere on the line. Now that we have created a third point (our midpoint), how do we *use it* to darken or lighten the image? Instead of dragging to the *left* and the *right* (as in Levels), in *Curves* you drag the points *up* and *down*. Dragging *down* (4) makes the Value point *darker*, and dragging *up* (5) makes it *lighter*. We can see all points are connected with a smooth curved line.

I will place another point, and drag it up to brighten the image in the *darker* areas (6).

You can delete a point again by dragging it out of the window, at the *left* or *right* (7) side.

If there is a specific *area* in the image you want to adjust, for example the sky, you can add a point by *Shift-clicking* on this area (8).

An *easy* way to *move* a point is by using the *up* and *down* arrow keys. To move a point in larger steps, hold down the *Shift* key while using the *up* and *down* arrow keys. To select *another point* on the curve, you can use the *left* and *right* arrow keys.

You can also make the window larger, by dragging at a corner or side (9).

As with Levels, in Curves you can also adjust the *individual color channels*. This way, you can do sophisticated color corrections by adjusting the *individual* curves of the three color channels.

In the next lesson we will look at Brightness-contrast.

18. Brightness-Contrast

In this lecture we will look at *Brightness-Contrast*, and the special relationship between *Brightness-contrast*, *Levels* and *Curves*. Open *Tree.xcf*. Here we see the bark of a tree. The image looks a bit flat (1). It could use some more contrast. Go to: *Colors > Brightness-Contrast*. I increase the contrast a bit, to 30 (2). You can also do this by holding the mouse above the slider, and scroll. To compare, click on *Preview*.

I you click on: *Edit these Settings as Levels* (3), *Levels* opens (4). Levels now shows what actually happened when we increased the contrast. The dark tones have been darkened (5), and the light tones have been lightened (6). The midtones have stayed unchanged. In *Levels*, I can click on *Edit these Settings as Curves*. Now I can see how my contrast adjustment looks like in *Curves* (7). I click on Cancel.

I open *Brightness-Contrast* again. I will now go the other way, and *reduce* the contrast by dragging the slider to the left. This results in a more flat, greyish image. To see what happened, click on *Edit these Settings as Levels* (8).

We can see that now the *Output* Levels sliders are brought inwards, making dark less dark, and light less light (9).

Click on *Edit these Settings as Curves* (10). This is how the contrast adjustment looks like in *Curves* (11). I click on Cancel.

I open *Brightness-Contrast* one more time. We will now include the *Brightness* slider. When I increase the contrast, let's say to 40, the image gets lighter (12). I can adjust for this by *decreasing* the *Brightness* (13).

Click on *Edit these Settings as Levels*. What *Brightness* has done, is it has shifted *all three sliders* equally to the right, the midtone slider included (14).

To conclude, *Brightness-Contrast* is a quick and easy way to improve images that lack contrast. To fine-tune the result, you can go to *Levels* or *Curves*.

In the next lesson, we will look at Hue-Saturation.

19. Hue-Saturation

As the name implies, with *Hue-Saturation* you can adjust two of the three color components; *Hue* and *Saturation*. In fact, you can even adjust *Value*, but not in the advanced way as you can with *Levels* or *Curves*. Each tool has its own speciality and unique way of working.
Open *Organ.jpg*.

Let's first look at *Saturation*. I would like to adjust the saturation of this image. To open *Hue-Saturation*, go to *Colors > Hue-Saturation*. I would like to bring a bit more color into this image. When you increase *Saturation*, you will shift pastel tints more to saturated colors. To do this, drag the *Saturation* slider to the right (1). If you toggle the *Preview*, you'll see the colors have come a bit more to life.

Hue-Saturation can also be used for color adjustments.
Click on *Reset* (2) to undo earlier settings. On top the color wheel is represented (3). The complementary color of *Red* (R), meaning the color on the *other side* of the color circle, is *Cyan* (C).
The complementary color of *Green* (G) is *Magenta* (M).
And the complementary color of *Blue* (B) is *Yellow* (Y).
In Hue-saturation you can *rotate* the color wheel. If you rotate, you're shifting the *Hue's*. You can do this for all colors at the same time, but also for *individual* colors.

Let's say I want to make the pipes of the organ more blue.
Because the pipes are Cyan, I select *Cyan* (4) in the color wheel. I can now rotate the color wheel in two directions; *clockwise* and *counter clockwise*. If you rotate the color wheel clockwise, you'll move all *Cyan* colors to the direction of *Green*, *Yellow*, or *Red*. And if you go *counter clockwise*, you'll move *Cyan* colors in the direction of *Blue*, *Magenta*, and *Red*. So to shift *Cyan* to *Blue*, you go *counter clockwise*. To do this, drag the *Hue slider* to the right (5).

The image changes as you drag. And in the color wheel, you can see the *Cyan* thumbnail has been changed to *Blue* (6). Click on *Preview* to compare (7, 8). Then click on OK.
Let's look at a second example. Open *Mountains.jpg*.

Let's make the red leaves green. I open *Hue-Saturation*. To adjust the red leaves, I select *Red (R)* in the color wheel. To shift *Red* to *Green*, we go counter clockwise. I can drag the Hue *slider* to the right, but I can also fill in *degrees* manually. A single color shift (for example from *Red* to *Yellow*) is *60 degrees*. Shifting *two* colors is *120 degrees*, and going to the complementary color on the other side, is *180 degrees*. I want to shift *two* colors, so a *120 degree* shift. I select the text inside the *Hue* entry field, type *120*, and press Enter.

As we can see, right now *not all* our reds have changed (9). To adjust how *many* red *tints* are affected, you use *Overlap*. Increasing Overlap (10) will *expand* the range of red colors that are shifted. As you drag Overlap to the right, more and more red tints will become green (11). We've now also made the roof of the house green. To deal with this use a layer mask (lesson 28). And *advanced* ways of selecting are discussed in the *Google Nik collection* chapter. All leaves are green now, but a bit too saturated. So I will *decrease* the *Saturation* by dragging the slider to the left. To get a better color match with the other green leaves in the image, I will shift the color a bit more to yellow, and set *Hue* to *90 degrees*. We've now changed red leaves into green leaves.

For the last example open *Girl.jpg*. The girl wears a blue shirt. Let's make the shirt darker. Click on *Blue (B)* in the color wheel. Increase *Overlap* to include all blue tints. Now I drag *Lightness* to the left to darken the shirt. I'll also decrease the *Saturation* a bit. To change the *color* of the shirt, drag the *Hue* slider.

In the next lesson we will look at the Color Picker.

20. Using the Color Picker

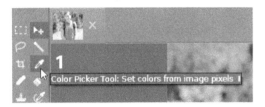

With the *Color Picker* you can sample or pick a color from your image. Open *Girl.jpg*. Select the *Color Picker* tool (1). If you click on the shirt (2), the *Foreground color* will show the sampled color.

If you *Shift-click* on the image, the *Color Picker window* opens (3). On the left there are the *Red*, *Green* and *Blue* values. And at the right, Red, Green and Blue are shown as *percentages*.

You can also show *Hue*, *Saturation* and *Value* if you want to (4). If you *drag* in your image you'll see the color information directly updated.

When you hold the mouse button down, you see a little *white square*. Let's zoom in to see the square better (5). The color you sample with the *Color Picker*, is an *average* of the pixels that are *inside* the square. The reason for this, is that pixels laying next to each other can *differ* quite a bit. Taking an *average* of a couple of pixels will give a more reliable result.

The size of the square can be adjusted in the *Tool Options*. The *Radius* (of the square) is now set to 5. A *Radius* of 5 means we'll get an 11 by 11 pixel *square*. This is also a default size in Photoshop. To change the *Radius*, you can scroll inside the Radius bar. If you want to sample just a *single* pixel, *uncheck Sample average*.

Sample merged (7) means, that *all layers* are looked at, when you click somewhere. So not just the active layer is measured, but *all visible layers*. This means you're measuring what you're actually seeing.

In the next lesson we will look at how to save a file with layers.

21. Saving work file

To save a file that has layers, you save it in Gimp's native *.xcf* format. You can later open this 'work' file again, and continue working with the layers. To save a work file, go to: *File > Save As*. The *Save Image* window opens (1). At the top you can give your file a name (2), and at the left you can navigate to the folder where you want to save (3). Then click on Save.

If you want to create a new folder, you can do this by clicking on the *Create Folder*

button at the top right (4). As we saw earlier, you can also (5) *bookmark* a folder. Bookmarked folders are time savers for *both*

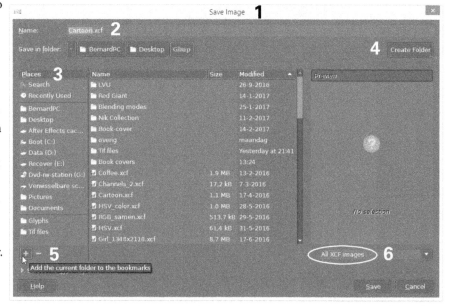

opening and saving files. Because we are saving in Gimps native format, Gimp by default only shows existing *.xcf* files that are in a folder. If you want to see all the images in a folder, click at the bottom right on: *All XCF images* (6), and choose: *All images* (7). To see all content of a folder, choose above: *All files*.

In chapter 4 we will look at saving images for the Web, for Print, saving as a PDF, and saving as a Photoshop file.

In the next chapter we will look at making selections.

Chapter 3

Making selections

22. The Rectangle and Ellipse select tool

In this lecture, we'll look at the *Rectangle* and *Ellipse* select tool. If I want to brighten up the sky in a landscape, and leave the *rest* of the image untouched, I need a way to *select* the sky. In this chapter we will look at different ways to make a selection. We will start with two elementary, but important selection tools: the *Rectangle* and the *Ellipse* select tool. They can be found at the top left and bottom left of the *Tool bar*.
Let's create a new document. Go to: *File > New*. Make it 800 by 500 pixels. Click on the *Rectangle* tool at the top, or press *M*.

To draw a selection, *drag* over the canvas. You can recognize a selection because of the 'marching ants', as they are called. The marching ants define the *border* of the selection. Everything that is *inside* the selection, is *selected*, everything that is *outside* the selection, is *not selected*. Now that we have a selection, what can we do with it? Let's open *Levels* by going to: *Colors > Levels*. If I now drag the white *output* slider to the left, only the pixels inside the selection will be darkened. The pixels outside the selection are unaffected. Click on Cancel.
To *stop* a selection, go to: *Select > None*, or press *Ctrl-D*. The *D* in *Ctrl-D*, stands for 'De-select'. The marching ants are gone, and there is no selection anymore.

Let's explore the *Rectangle* tool a bit further. Drag a selection again. You can now *change* the *size* of the selection by dragging at the sides, or by dragging at the corners.

To get rounded corners, in the *Tool Options*, click on *Rounded corners* (1). With *Radius* you determine the *size* of the rounded corners. Press *Ctrl-D* to deselect.

Now let's have a look at the *Ellipse* select tool, which is at the bottom left of the toolbar. Click on it, and drag an ellipse. Here we can also change it's size by dragging at the sides and the corners. Press *Ctrl-D* to deselect.

To daw a *circle*, first start dragging, and then add the *Shift* key (2). Keep the *Shift* key pressed down. When you're finished dragging, *first* release the mouse button, and then release the *Shift* key. This works the same for the *Rectangle* select tool to create a square.

You can also *move* your selection, by dragging *inside* the selection. Clicking inside the selection *without moving* the selection, is the same as pressing *Enter*. This will turn the *adjustable* selection into a *normal* selection (3). A normal selection cannot be adjusted by dragging at the sides or the corners. However, when you click *inside* the selection *again* with the *Rectangle* (or *Ellipse*) select tool, you will be able to drag the sides and corners again (4).

If you have made a selection, and then press *Shift*, at the right of the cursor you will see a *small plus sign* appearing (5). By holding down *Shift*, you can now *add another* selection (6). You can move *and* adjust the second selection *independent* of the first selection. If you want to *merge* the two selections *together*, drag the new selection over the first selection (7). You can now still do some last adjustments to it (8), and when you want to merge, press *Enter* (9).

Now the two selections have merged to one selection.

You can also *subtract* from a selection. If you press *Ctrl*, at the right of the cursor you will see a *small minus sign* appearing (10). With *Ctrl* pressed down, drag a new selection (11). You can drag the new selection *over* the existing selection. You can make some last adjustments (12), and press *Enter* (13). You have now *subtracted* from the selection.

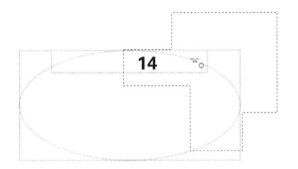

You can also make an *intersection*. Let's use the *Ellipse* select tool for this. Press *Shift plus Ctrl*, and drag *over* the existing selection. You can make some last adjustments (14), and then press *Enter*. Now you made an *intersection* of the two selections (15).

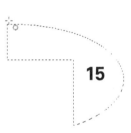

You can *undo* selection changes, by pressing *Ctrl-Z*. Each selection change is a *separate* state in the *History* panel.

Now we've seen how to create different shapes with selections, in the next lesson we will look at the Free select tool.

23. The Free select tool

With the *Free select* tool, you can freely draw selection shapes by hand. Click on the *Free select* tool that looks like a *lasso* (1).

To draw a shape, drag (2), and when you return to the beginning of your selection, you will see a yellow circle (3). When your mouse is above the yellow circle, release your mouse, and the selection *closes*.

Another way to draw with the Free select tool is by *clicking*. Press *Ctrl-D* to deselect. Click once on the canvas to start a new selection. If you now move your mouse you'll get a *straight line*. Click again, and move your mouse again. To make a *horizontal* or *vertical* line (4), press the *Ctrl* key. Another way to close a selection, is by double-clicking. From wherever you double-click, you will *close* the selection with a straight line.

You can *both* drag *and* click interchangeably, while making a selection.

As with the *Rectangle* and *Ellipse* select tool, you can *add* to the selection, or *subtract* from it. And this is where the Free select tool is often used for. With the Free select tool you can quickly correct and optimize an existing selection. When you hold down *Shift*, you *add* to the selection (5). And when you hold down *Ctrl*, you *subtract* from the selection (6).

So with the *Free select tool*, you can quickly make a selection in any form.

In the next lesson, we will discover the Path tool, which is the tool for making professional selections.

24. The Paths tool

The contour of real world objects such as people, flowers, or cars, exists of mainly curved lines. To accurately select these curves, we use the *Paths* tool. The *Paths* tool can be found at the left side of the *Text* tool (1). Open *Sine.xcf*.

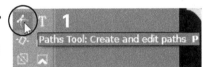

We'll explore the paths tool by drawing over a curved line. I start at the top left. I click and hold the mouse button down (2). Now I drag a bit to the right (3). What I just did is, I placed a point (which is the circle in the middle) and by dragging I pulled *out* of the circle *two arms*. The circle is the center, and the arms can be *rotated* around it. The arms can also be pulled out and pulled in.

The function of the arms is to give the line we are going to draw *curvature*. Let's place a second point at the bottom of the sine. Click (4), and drag to the right again (5). As we see, by dragging out the arms, we're adjusting the curvature of the line.

Release the mouse button. If you want to, you can now move *each* arm *individually* (6).
And when you press *Shift*, the arms will move as *one* again, mirrored in their origin point (the circle).

To *close* a path (7), press *Ctrl* (8) and click on the first placed point (9).

After closing a path you can *still* improve the path by dragging all points, and adjusting all arms.

Open *Circle.xcf*. To quickly draw a path around the circle, I will first place four points without dragging, one point at every 90 degrees (10). To help placing these four points, two lines are visible in the circle. To close the path, *Ctrl*-click on the first point. Next, add four *additional* points in the middle of the straight lines. To *add* a new point on a line, press *Ctrl*, and *click on the line* (11). A new point will be added. Drag the new point to the edge, about in the middle (12). To make the curve *fit* the circle, press *Shift* and drag the arms out just a bit further (13).

Also do this for the other three lines (14). Now our path is finished.

After drawing a path, we want to get a *selection* from it. To turn a path into a *selection*, go to the *Paths* panel (15). Here you can see a thumbnail of the path you drew. Like in the layers panel, you can give the path a name. I call it *circle*.

To turn the path into a selection, click on the *Path to selection* icon (16). Now we see the marching ants again (17). You can *hide* the path (so you will *only* see the *selection*) by clicking on the *Move* tool (18). Deselect by pressing *Ctrl-D*. To make the *path* visible again, and *automatically* also select the *Path* tool, just *double*-click on the path *thumbnail*.

Now let's create a *second* path, by *Shift*-clicking on the *Create a new path* icon (19). I draw a simple triangle, partly *over* the circle, and close the path by *Ctrl*-clicking on the first point (20). In the Paths panel, when you *Alt*-click on the *circle thumbnail*, éven though this path is *not* selected *or* visible, *Alt*-clicking will give you it's selection. Like with the *Rectangle* and *Ellipse* select tools, you can *add*, *subtract*, or *intersect* with a second selection, *now* coming from a *path*. This means we can *add* the *triangle* selection *to* the circle selection by *Shift-Alt* clicking on the triangle thumbnail (21).

We have now *added* the *triangle* to the *circle*, as a selection (22).

Let's also do an *intersection*. I create a third path by *Shift*-clicking on the *Create a new path* icon. I draw a *rectangle*, partly over the circle (23). To get an intersection of this *rectangle* with the *selection*, press *Shift-Ctrl-Alt*, and click on the *rectangle* thumbnail. To hide the path and *only* see the selection, click on the *Move* tool (24).

Now let's practice with a real image. Open *Coffee.xcf*. Let's say, in this image I would like to change the *color* of the background, but I want to leave the mug unchanged.

To do this I will select the mug by drawing a path around it. When the mug is selected, I will cut out the mug, and place the isolated mug on a separate layer on top. If I then change the color of the layer below, the mug won't be affected, because it has been placed on a separate layer.

Select the *Paths* tool, and zoom in to about 400%. Here I recognize a *sine wave form* (25). I will click and drag my first point at the top of the sine (26). Then I click and drag at the bottom of the sine (27). To make the curve fit, I adjust the arms. The direction and length of the arms, will form of the curve.

After adjusting, when you want to continue drawing, the *last placed point* has to be the *active point*. An active point has a *transparent* circle, instead of a circle filled with *white*. So when the last placed point is white, and you want to continue drawing, *click* on the last point to make it active (transparent). Then you can continue drawing.

I click and drag a new point, and adjust the handles again (28).

When the distance between two points gets longer, the curve often will be more difficult to draw. However, placing points too close to each other, also isn't effective and

will be time-consuming. With a little practice, you will quickly start to recognize the *natural* existing *sine forms*, so you won't draw more curves than needed, and you won't try to draw several curves at the same time.

For larger areas I personally use the method I used for drawing the circle.

I click (so without dragging) to set a new point (29). At the place, where there is the *most* distance between my line, and the edge of the object, I will *Ctrl*-click to place a new point (30). Then I drag this point to the edge. To *continue* drawing, *first* click on the *last* point to make it active.

After finishing, we have a path *around* the mug. We however should not forget the *inside* of the handle. Drawing a new path, *inside* a path, will automatically *exclude* this area from the selection (31). Now our path is complete (32).

In the Paths panel *Alt*-click on the thumbnail, to turn the path into a selection (33). Press *V* to select the *Move* tool, so you only see the selection (34).

Now open the layers panel. To place the mug on a new layer, press *Ctrl-J*. After pressing *Ctrl-J*, the selection is gone, and the content of the selection is placed on a new layer, *above* the layer that was active. The new layer will have the name: *Layer via Copy*, and it will be the active layer.

In the Layers panel, you are *also* able to *Alt*-click on a layer thumbnail. The selection you get will come from the *existing pixels* that are on that layer. *Alt*-clicking on the *Layer via Copy* layer, will give the same selection as *Alt*-clicking on the mug *path*. Also, like in the Paths panel, a layer *doesn't* have to be selected *or* visible, to get a selection from it.

In the *Layers* panel we're also able to *add*, *subtract*, and *intersect* selections (based on the existing pixels on a layer). The same key combinations are used: *Shift-Alt* clicking will *add* the pixels of a layer to the selection. *Ctrl-Alt*-clicking will *subtract* the pixels of a layer, from the selection. *Shift-Ctrl-Alt* clicking will give an *intersection* of the pixels on a layer, and the selection.

I make a circle selection (35).

Then I *Shift-Alt*-click on the mug layer, to *add* the selection of the mug.

I make a circle selection again. Now I *Ctrl-Alt*-click on the mug layer, to *subtract* the mug *from* the *circle* selection (37).

I make a circle selection again. Now I *Shift-Ctrl-Alt*-click on the mug layer, to make an *intersection* of the *mug* and the *circle* selection (38). Deselect by pressing *Ctrl-D*.

With *Ctrl-J* we placed the mug on a separate layer, *above* the background. So I can now change the color of the background, without affecting the mug.

In the next lesson we'll explore how to select color.

25. The Select by color tool

In this lesson we will look at how to make a selection based on *color*.

In the toolbox there are *two* color select tools. They both do the same thing: they make selections based on color *similarity*. The *Fuzzy select* tool (1) looks for similar colors *adjacent* to where you click. The *Select by color* tool (2) looks *everywhere* in the image to find similar colors. Open *Coffee.xcf*. The *Fuzzy select* tool, known as the 'Magic Wand tool' in Photoshop, is located below the *Move* tool. Let's see if we can select the mug with the *Fuzzy select* tool. When you click somewhere on the mug, the tool will select colors that are *similar* to the color you clicked on. How different a color has to be before it is included in the selection, is set under *Threshold* in the *Tool Options*. The *higher* the Threshold, the *more* colors that will be included in the selection, and the *larger* the area of the selection will become. An efficient way to increase the Threshold is by dragging *inside the image*.

When you drag *inside the mug* (3), in the *Tool Options* the Threshold is going up (4). And as the Threshold is going up, more and more pixels are added to the selection. At some point however, the selection will go *outside* the mug (5). In an ideal situation, you would be able select the whole mug, before the selection goes outside the mug. However, objects in the real world are not always that easy to select by their color. With a partial selection the question arises: should I *use* this selection I have, and try to *improve* it, or am I better off by drawing a *path*? A third possibility is using the **Nik collection** which is specialised in making professional selections. We'll look at the Nik collection in chapter 5.

Open *Sky.jpg*. Let's say we want to select the sky. If you use the *Fuzzy select* tool and you drag in the sky, you're *not* selecting the blue sky *between* the *branches* of the tree (6). This is because the Fuzzy select tool only selects *connected* pixels, starting from the place where you start dragging. The other color selection tool is the *Select by Color* Tool. For the *Select by Color* tool, similar colors *don't* have to be connected, so you can get multiple selections. Click on the *Select by Color* tool. If you now drag in the image, the blue sky between the branches is also selected (7).

Fuzzy select

Select by Color

To include the cloud at the left, I use the *Free Select* tool.

To *add* to the selection, press the *Shift* key and click once. After having placed the first point, you can release the *Shift* key. Click around the cloud. You can also click *outside* the image, to include everything (8).

When you close the selection, you have *added* the cloud *to* the selection (9). With the selection loaded press *Ctrl-J*. Ctrl-J will place the selected sky on a separate layer (10).
You can now adjust the sky.

If you need a *selection* of the sky again, you can *Alt*-click on the sky layer thumbnail. And when you need a new layer with the *original* sky, click on the background and press *Ctrl-J* again.

In the next lecture we'll look at ways to improve a selection.

26. How to improve selections

In this lecture, we will *improve* the selection we get from the mug, using the skills we have learned so far. Open *Coffee.xcf*.

Select the mug again (1), by dragging inside the mug (2) and selecting as much of the mug as possible (3). Now we will improve the selection, and use various methods for this.

There are three areas where we have to *add* to the selection. And *below* the mug the selection went outside the mug, so we have to *remove* the selection area there. To remove a big piece of a selection, you can use the *Rectangle select* tool. Press *Ctrl* to *subtract* from the selection, and start dragging from under the image up until the mug (4). Then press Enter (5).

Now select the *Free select* tool. Let's add the top of the mug to the selection. Press the *Shift* key to add, and click inside the selection (6). After placing the first point, you can release the *Shift* key.

Now go over the top of the mug, to add it to the selection (7). Because the *Free select* tool is unable to draw curves, you have to draw the curve at the top by placing several short distanced points (8).

When you have reached the inside of the selection again (9), you can close the selection, for example by double-clicking (10).

Because the *Free select* tool can't draw curves, I will now use the *Paths* tool to correct the bottom of the mug.

I select the *Paths* tool. I start the path somewhere outside the selection (11). To make a curve for the bottom, I place a point at the other side (12). Then I press *Ctrl*, and click in the middle to add a point. I drag the point to the edge (13). Then I hold *Shift* so I can move *both* arms at the same time, and drag the arms *out* to get the right curvature. I click on the end point to continue. To finish the path, I go outside the selection again (14). I close the path by *Ctrl*-clicking on the first point (15). I go to the *Paths* panel. I *subtract* the path from the selection, by *Ctrl-Alt* clicking on the path thumbnail. I press *V* to see the result (16).

You can also turn a *selection*, into a *path* (and then adjust the *path* instead of the selection). At the right side of the *Path to selection* icon, we have it's *opposite*: the *Selection to path* icon (17). When you click on it you get a new path, called: Selection (18). Double-click on the path thumbnail, and deselect the selection by pressing *Ctrl-D*.

I zoom in on the path that was created from the selection. I can reposition points (19), and I can adjust the handles (20). Hold down *Ctrl* to be able to pull out the arms, when they are still *inside* a circle.

You can also *delete* points by selecting them, and pressing *Backspace*. When you're finished adjusting the path, *Alt*-click on the path thumbnail, to get a new selection. Press *V* to select the *Move* tool. Go to the *Layers* panel, and place the Mug on a new layer, by pressing *Ctr-J*.

In the next lesson we will look at a powerful way to select: *painting* selections.

27. The Quick mask

Another way to make a selection, is by *painting* it. This is very useful for isolating objects that don't have a *hard edge*. Let's have a look. Open *Monkeys.jpg*. Because of the fur, the monkeys have a soft transition to the background. Drawing a path would be very difficult, and also *wouldn't* give a satisfactory result. For selecting soft edges, you use the *Quick mask*.

To prepare for the *Quick mask*, I will first make a *rough* selection with the *Free select* tool, at the outside of the monkeys (1). By holding down the mouse, I can quickly draw around them.

To go to the *Quick mask*, click at the bottom left on the little circle icon (2). You can also press *Q*. By pressing *Q*, you will toggle between *Quick mask mode*, and *selection mode*. In Quick mask mode you can now clearly see the *inside*, and the *outside* of the selection (3). The monkeys are at the *inside* the selection. Everything that's outside the selection, is coloured *red*. Like in Photoshop, *red* for the Quick mask is the default. But you can change this to another color, as we will see later.

Let's zoom in a bit, so we can clearly see the transition from the fur to the background. Select the *Paintbrush* tool, and select a soft brush with 0% hardness. Press *Alt* and scroll the brush size to around 60. Set the Fore- and Background to black and white, by pressing *D*. Painting with black will make the selection *smaller* (the *red* area is made bigger) and painting with white makes the selection *larger*. By pressing the *X* key, you can quickly *switch* between painting with black and painting with white. Let's start with black, to *hide* more of the background (4).

I will adjust the appearance of the mask a bit, to better see what I am painting. I right-click on the Quick mask *icon* at the bottom left, and choose: *Configure Color and Opacity* (5). To adjust the *color* of the Quick mask, click on the rectangle at the right (6).

The *Edit Quick Mask Color* window will open (7). You can now adjust the *color* of the Quick mask. I my situation the *red* gives good contrast with the *green* background, so I will keep the red. I click on Cancel. What I will change is the Mask *opacity*. When I *increase* the Mask *opacity* (8), the Quick mask becomes *less* transparent. This helps me to better see the result of my painting.

I drag the opacity slider to about 70%, and click on OK.

When you remove too much fur (9), just press *X* to reverse the brush.
Then paint with white, to *increase* the selection again (10). At different places,
you can use different brush sizes. For example, around the *nose* (11) of the
right monkey, you can use a *smaller* brush, because there is almost no fur.

Finally (12), fill the gap with
a hard brush (13).

When you're finished (14),
press *Q* to go to *selection
mode*. Then press *Ctrl-J* to
place the selected monkeys
on a new layer (15).

In the next lecture, we will
look at a more flexible and
non-destructive alternative
for using *Ctrl-J*; the layer mask.

28. The Layer mask

Until now we have used *Ctrl-J* to place selected pixels on a separate layer. In this lecture, we will look at a *non-destructive* alternative for using *Ctrl-J*: the layer mask.

At the left side we see the *Ctrl-J* method (1). The bottom layer is the original image, shown with a selection around the monkeys (2). Pressing *Ctrl-J* will

give us the layer above (3), as we did in the last lectures. When we use *Ctrl-J*, we *copy* the pixels inside of the selection, and place these pixels on the layer above (3). The pixels *outside* the selection are discarded.

This is called *destructive*, because we are *losing* pixels from a layer. Losing pixels from a layer also means *losing the ability* to make *changes later on*. For example, if I later would decide I also want to show the *twig* the baby monkey is holding, I can't do that anymore on the *Layer via Copy* layer, because the pixels I need for this, are not available anymore. So ideally, I would leave *all* the existing pixels of a layer intact, when I *isolate* an object. I can do this, by using a layer *mask*, which is shown at the right (4).

A layer *mask* is a second, black and white image, that is *added* to a layer. A layer mask will *store the selection* that you make. Where the mask is *white*, you will see the *content* of the layer, and where the mask is *black*, the content of the layer is *hidden* (white *reveals*, black *conceals*). This way, no pixels have to be deleted. They are just *hidden* by the mask. The mask is very flexible, because you can show and hide content of a layer, *at any time*.

A layer mask can also have tints of *grey*. Where the mask is *grey*, the layer has *transparency*. A darker grey (5) means *more* transparency, so the content here will only be slightly visible (6). And a lighter grey (7) means *less* transparency, so the content will be more visible (8) but is still transparent, so *you can still* see through it.

If I now want to add the *twig* that the baby monkey is holding, I am able to do that by changing the *black* pixels on the layer mask, to *white* pixels. This will reveal the twig. I could draw a *path* around the twig, turn that path into a *selection*, and fill the selection with *white*, *inside* the layer mask, which reveals the twig.

Open *Monkeys_twig.xcf*. Here *Ctrl-J* has been used to create the top layer. At the bottom we have the original layer. On the original layer, we are going to place a layer mask. First *Alt*-click on the top layer to get a *selection* from it's pixels. Then *right-click* on the bottom layer, and choose: *Add Layer Mask* (9). We want to make a mask from the *selection*, so click on *Selection* (10). Then press Enter.

We can now see, an extra black and white thumbnail has been added at the right side of the content thumbnail (11). The black and white mask has now *stored* our selection, so you can safely *deselect* the selection by pressing *Ctrl-D*. The *Ctrl-J* layer and *mask* layer now *visually* show exactly the same content. However, on the *Ctrl-J* layer the non-visible pixels have been *deleted*, and on the *mask* layer the non-visible pixels are just *hidden*, and can be revealed at any time.

To add the twig, I've already made a path. Go to the *Paths* panel, and *Alt*-click on the twig thumbnail to turn the path into a selection. Go back to the *Layers* panel. To add the twig, make sure that the black and white *mask* is *selected*. You can see whether the mask is selected, by the *white border* around the mask thumbnail (11). The layer *content* thumbnail now has a *black border* (11), which indicates it is *not* selected.

If you click on the *content* thumbnail, you'll see the white border is now around the *content* thumbnail (12). Click on the *mask* again (13). To fill the mask with white (coming from the selection) press *Ctrl-Backspace* (14). Press *Ctrl-D* to deselect. We now made the twig *visible* on the content layer (15).

You can also *paint* on the mask. Let's say we want to *remove* a leaf (16). Press B to select the brush, and select a soft brush. Set the size to about 50.

Check that the *mask* is selected, so that you're not painting with black on the *content*. Paint with *black*, to *hide* pixels. When you now paint over the leaf (17), you are hiding it. This is because you're making white pixels black, inside the layer mask. Now let's *add* a leave.

To add a leave, I would like to have the background *visible* again, like I had with the *Quick mask*. To *simulate* the Quick mask, duplicate the layer with the layer mask. *Right-click* on the bottom layer mask layer, and choose: *Delete Layer Mask. Shift*-click on the *Create a new layer* button. Click on the Foreground color, select red, and click on OK. Press *Alt-Backspace* to fill the layer with red (18). Set the Opacity of the red layer, to 50% (19). Now click on the layer mask of the top layer (20). The Quick mask has now been simulated.

Like with the Quick mask, painting with *black* will make the selection *smaller*, and painting with *white* will make the selection *larger*. Press *D* to set the Fore- and Background to black and white. We can now easily *reveal* a leaf, because we're able to *see* the *hidden* pixels (because we placed the original image below, tinted red by a transparent red layer above it).

I'll paint with white, inside the *mask*. To get white press *X*, to switch the Fore- and Background color. I zoom in on the image to about 400%. Probably the easiest way to add a leaf, is by first *roughly* revealing what you want to add (so making *more* visible than is needed). Then (as we did with the monkeys) paint backwards with *black* towards the edge. At any time, you can *check* the result, by *Shift-clicking* on the eye of the top layer, which will then hide the layers below. *Shift*-click again, to reveal all layers again. For fine-tuning, you could paint with only the top layer visible.

Because we only *simulated* the Quick mask, pressing *Q* now *won't* give me a selection. To get a *selection* from the *mask*, *right-click* on the layer, and choose: *Mask to Selection* (21).

You can *hide* the mask, so temporarily disable it, by *Ctrl*-clicking on the mask (22). You can *see* a mask is *disabled*, when it has a *red* border around it. *Ctrl*-click on the mask again, to activate it again.

As you can hide a *mask*, you can also hide the *content* of a layer, so you only see the mask. To only see the mask, you *Alt*-click on the mask (23).

This can be useful to *check* the mask for small *mistakes*. Looking only at the mask, you can quickly see if you have missed a spot somewhere (24). You can *see* the *content* is hidden, when the mask shows a *green* border. *Alt*-click on the mask again to reveal the content again.

In the next lesson we will look at several common uses of layer masks.

29. Uses of Layer masks

Masks have many uses. They can for example be used for *Color* and *Value* corrections.

Open *Girl_Close-up.xcf*. Let's say I would like to remove the greenish color tint around the girls mouth (1). To do this, I first *duplicate* the layer, and then open *Curves*. I go to the *Green* channel (2).

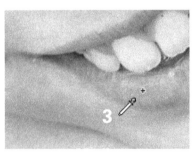

I now *Shift*-click (3) on the greenish skin. This will place a point in the Green channel at the *Value level* I want to adjust (4). Now I move the placed point *down* a bit, to *remove* green at this Value level (5). You can also use the *down* arrow key to lower the point (it's a bit easier than using the mouse). I click on OK.

Next, add a layer *mask* to the color adjusted layer. *Right-click* on the layer and choose *Add Layer Mask*. Choose *Black* for the color of the mask, so that you will start with *hiding* the complete layer (6). Press Enter. The layer is now hidden.

Press *B* to select the brush. Press *X* to paint with *white*, so you will *reveal* the pixels of the color corrected layer. Select a soft brush with 0% hardness. *Alt*-scroll to set the size to around 70. Now paint with a very *low brush opacity*. If you do this, you're able to *gradually* remove the green tint. Set the opacity of the brush to about 10% (7). With each paint stroke, you're

removing a bit of green where you paint, because you're *slowly adding* the color of the adjusted layer. This way you're flexible in *how much* green you want to remove. At those places where you removed too *much* green you can

reverse the process by pressing *X*, and painting with *black*.

When you're satisfied with the result, you can *merge* the two layers back into *one* layer. You can do this by *right-clicking* on the top layer and choose: *Merge Down* (8). The shortcut for merging down is *Ctrl-E* (see also: *Layer > Merge Down*). We've now color corrected the image with the use of a layer *mask*.

Now we will look at *dodging and burning*, where we adjust the *Value* levels of an image, using layer masks. Make two copies of the layer you want to adjust (9). We will make one layer *darker*, and the other layer *lighter*. Open *Curves* to darken the top layer. Drag the curve down a bit, and click on OK. Call the layer 'darken'. Hide the top layer, and select the layer below. Open *Curves* again, to lighten this layer. Drag the curve up a bit, and click on OK. Call the layer 'lighten'.

Now we will *hide* both Value adjusted layers with a (black) layer *mask*. *Right-click* on the layers, choose *Add Layer Mask*, choose *Black* for the color of the mask, and press Enter (10). Next select the brush. Choose a *soft* brush and increase the size to about 300. In the *Tool Options*, set the brush *Opacity* to around 30%. By painting inside the mask of the *darken* layer, you can *darken* areas. And when you paint inside the mask of the *lighten* layer, you can make areas *lighter* (11).

A last example I want to show you, is the use of a layer mask in combination with *text*. Open *Chicago.xcf*. In this document we have on top a *text* layer (12). Using text will be discussed in the next chapter. Below, we have an image of a city. And on the bottom

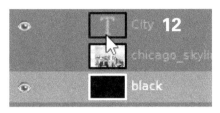

we have a layer filled with black. What I would like, is to have the image of the city visible, *inside* the letters.

To do this, first *Alt*-click on the text layer to get a *selection* of the text (13). Then *right-click* on the Chicago layer, and choose *Add Layer Mask* (14).

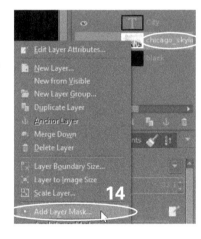

Click on *Selection*, and press Enter. Now you can deselect.

Hide the text layer, and reveal the Chicago layer (15).

You can also *move* the mask. By moving the *mask*, you can reveal *another* part of the city, showing inside the text (16). So make sure the *mask* is *selected* (has a *white* border around it) when you drag using the Move tool. If you *hide* the black layer, you can see the transparency created by the mask (17).

In the next lesson, we will look at selecting Channels.

30. Selecting Channels

In this lecture we'll look at how to make a selection from a Channel. Open *Channels.xcf*. I go to the *Channels* panel and set the size of the thumbnails to Enormous.

We have seen that layer masks are *black and white* images. The same is true for the Channels. The *Red*, *Green*, and *Blue* Channels are also *black and white* images. As we'll see in the next lesson where we will select hair, sometimes the information of a specific *Channel* can be very useful.

We see the numbers 1, 2, and 3. Each number is placed in a *separate* Channel. To turn the *Red* Channel (the 1) into a selection, *right-click* on it, and choose: *Channel to Selection* (1).

As we can see here, pure *black* pixels (in our case the number 1) aren't *included* in the selection (2). This is because in a selection, pure black *doesn't* have *any* transparency. As we saw with masks, *grey* pixels *do* have transparency. And white pixels are fully transparent. So *only* pure *black* pixels hide *completely*, and this is visually indicated by *excluding* black from the selection.

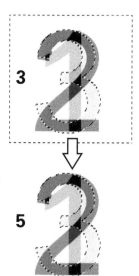

Let's say I want to use the *selection* of the *blue* channel (the 3), for making a layer *mask*. *Right-click* on the blue channel, and choose: *Channel to Selection* (3). To clearly see what is *inside* and what is *outside* the selection, you can also press *Q* to enter *Quick mask mode*. We see everything is selected, *except* the number 3 (because only the 3 is red). Press *Q* again to see the selection again.

I want the number 3 as a selection, so I will need to turn the selection *around*; I need to *invert* the selection. To do this, I go to: *Select > Invert* (4). Now the number 3 is selected (5).

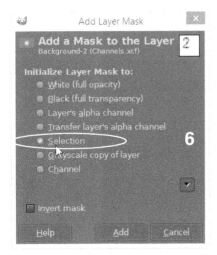

We have now made a *selection* of the blue channel, and we have *inverted* this selection.

Now, let's put the selection in to a layer *mask*. *Right*-click on the layer and choose: *Add Layer Mask*. Click on *Selection* (6), and press Enter. Press *Ctrl-D* to deselect. The layer mask is ready (7).

In the next lesson we will use this method to select hair.

31. Selecting hair

In this lesson we'll look at how to select hair. Open *Girl_hair.xcf*. To select hair, we need to find the best contrast we can get, between the hair and its surroundings. To find the best contrast, we will compare the three Channels. Go to the *Channels* panel, and set the thumbnails of the Channels to Gigantic. In our case, even at Gigantic, I think the thumbnails are too small to clearly see the hair. A quick way to see the three Channels at 100% is by going to: *Colors > Components > Decompose*. Click on OK.

Gimp has made a new document, where the channels are now visible as *layers*, called red, green, and blue (1). Press *Ctrl-1* for a 100% view.

Now let's *compare* the layers to find the one that gives the *best contrast* between the hair and it's surroundings. I think the blue layer gives the best contrast (2). So I will *drag* this layer *over* (3) to my original document (4). To do this, first drag the layer *on the thumbnail* of the original document, and then drag it *under the thumbnail*. We've now transferred a *layer* from one document, to another document.

We have now two layers: a *color* layer on the bottom (5), and a *black and white* layer (which is the *blue* channel!) on top (6). We will use the *blue channel* layer, as a *mask* for the *color* layer. Masks and channels are both black and white, so this matches.

Before we can use the blue channel layer as a mask, we first have to adjust it. The *background* has to become completely *black*, so that as a mask, it will *hide* everything that's around the girl. And the girl itself has to become completely *white*, so she will be completely *visible*.

Right now however, the *hair* of the girl is *much darker* than the background (7). For this reason it is often easier to initially work the other way around. We will *first* make the girl and her hair black, and the background white. When we're finished refining the layer we will *invert* the layer (turn it into a negative), so black becomes white, and white becomes black. Then the layer is ready to be used as a mask.

Creating a mask is normally done by boosting up the contrast a lot, and so forcing pixels in the *hair area* to become *either* back, *or* white. We want the hair to be completely black, and the background to be completely white.

This is best done with Levels. Go to: Colors > Levels. To make the background white, we'll use the *white point picker* (8). Click on the background, and drag. We're looking for a point, where the background becomes as white as possible, while still retaining *as much* hair as possible (9). The trade-off lies in the amount of cleaning up we will have to do afterwards.

Retaining *more hair*, normally has the consequence of having to do *more cleaning up*.

Next select the *black point picker* (10). Click at the top on the hair, and slowly drag to the edge (11). We're trying to find the *optimal* point, where the hair is *best defined*. Then click on OK.

Now that we have defined the blacks and the whites, it's time for the cleaning up. Select the brush. In the *Tool Options* select a brush with 100% hardness. *Alt*-scroll to set the size to 100.

We'll start with filling in the inside of the face, so we paint with black. Paint close, but not too close, along the edge of the hair (12).

Then zoom in (400%), and with a small *soft* brush, size 20, fill in the edge (13).

If you lower the *Opacity* of the layer to about 70% (14), you can see the original layer underneath, which helps with filling in the edge (15).

For painting the shoulders, I lower the Opacity even more (to about 30%) to clearly see the edge (16).

After painting the outline for the shoulders (17), I set the Opacity back to 100%. To fill in the rest of the girl with black (the shirt), I will now use the *free select* tool. I will click *in the middle* of the black line I drew on the shoulders (18).

When the selection is ready (19), I fill the selection with black, by pressing *Alt-Backspace*. Press *Ctrl-D* to deselect.

The black part is now ready (20).

The rest will be filled with white. To do this, we'll follow the same procedure. Draw with a small *soft* white brush alongside the finished black border (21), to clear the way for *drawing a selection* in the middle of it again.

For the outside, I will now use the *Paths* tool (22), which is a bit more flexible than the *Free select* tool.

Close the path by *Ctrl*-clicking on the first point (23).

Go to the *Paths* panel (24), and *Alt*-click on the path thumbnail to get a selection from it (25). Press *V* to select the *Move* tool.

At this moment, the *girl* is selected (bacause I made the path *around* the girl). In order to fill the *background* with white, I have to *invert* the selection.

Go to: *Select > Invert* (26). We've turned the selection around. Now I can fill the selection with *white*, by pressing *Alt-Backspace*. Press *Ctrl-D* to deselect (27).

27

To use this layer as a *mask*, we need to get a *selection* from it. Open the *Channels* panel. The layer we created is black and white, so the *Red*, *Green*, and *Blue* channels will be identical. It doesn't matter which channel we choose to make a selection from. I *right*-click on a Channel and choose: *Channel to Selection* (28). We now have a (Value) selection from our layer. Go back to the *Layers* panel. Right-click on the color layer and choose: *Add layer mask*. Click on *Selection*, and press Enter. Press *Ctrl-D* to deselect.

I hide the top layer. We can see I forgot to *invert* my selection (29). The background is now visible, and not the girl.

I did this, so I can show you that in stead of inverting a *selection*, you can also invert a *layer mask*. With the *mask* selected, go to *Colors > Invert* (30).

We've now *inverted* the mask, and see the girl (31).

Normally, a hair selection will have some *fringing*. *Fringing* means that when the subject that has been cut out, is placed against a *darker* background than it was *originally* in, at some places you will see a light *halo* around the hair. We will now *detect* and *remove* this fringing.

I will place the girl against a *black* background, so *all* existing halo's will become visible. I make a new layer, drag it behind the girl, and fill it with black. Now we can see where the halo's are (32).

Next, we'll remove the fringing by using a *blending mode*. Blending modes are discussed in the next chapter, but I already wanted to show you this trick here.

What the blending mode we're going to use will do, is *hide light* pixels (the fringing) when the image is placed in front of a *dark* background, and *show* the same light pixels, when the image is placed in front of a *light* background. With a light background, you can't see the fringing. And for a natural look, a bit of fringing in a light situation is even welcome. So the blending mode will make the image *adapt* itself to it's environment. As a result, the girl can be placed in front of any background.

We start with duplicating the color layer (33). Select the bottom color layer. Behind *Mode* (above *Opacity*), we see: *Normal* (34).
If you click on it, you get a list with blending modes. Choose: *Darken only* (35).

Now select the layer *mask*, of the *top* color layer. Zoom in to about 400%. Here we can clearly see the fringing (36). Select the brush. Choose a soft brush, size 20. Select black (to *hide* pixels). Paint over the halo's you want to remove (37). You can remove the fringing at those places where you think the fringing looks unnatural, when shown in front of a dark background. Some areas (like the top of the head) benefit from a bit softer transition to the background. You can do this by increasing the brush *size*, which will soften the transition.

Now let's have a look at what happens when the background becomes *lighter*. Select the black layer, and open *Levels*.

If you drag the black *Output* slider to the right, you'll see the *hidden* hair slowly *reappears*. To be able to *move* the girl, *link* the two layers, so they will move as one (38). How to remove objects like the hair we see on her right shoulder, is discussed in the Retouching chapter.

In the next lesson we will look at cropping an image.

Chapter 4

Cropping, Resizing, and more

32. Cropping

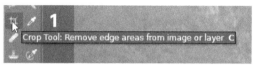

When you're cropping an image you're removing image space that you don't need.

Open *Girl_crop_original.jpg*. Let's say I want to cut out the girl. To do this, select the *Crop* tool (1).

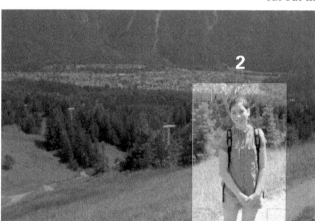

Now drag over the girl (2). The area that will be removed is darkened.

You can adjust the frame, by dragging at the sides and at the corners. You can also *move* the frame by dragging inside the frame. *Clicking once* inside the frame, so without dragging, will *crop* the image. Pressing Enter will also crop the image.

If you have a *specific* size in mind, select *Fixed* in the *Tool Options* (3). Whether you crop for use on *screen*, or whether you crop for *print*, in both cases you will be using *Aspect ratio*.

If you crop for the *screen* (for example for use on the *internet*), it could be that you need a 268 pixels wide, by 421 pixels high image. And in the case of *print*, the destination for your image could be a 4 by 6 inch *photo*. In *both* cases, you're dealing with a *Fixed Aspect ratio* (for *screen*: 268 to 241, for *print*: 4 to 6).

Let's start with the first example. We want an image of 268 pixels wide, and 421 pixels high for use on the internet. Beneath *Fixed*, we need both numbers, *separated* by a semicolon. So I select the text in the text entry field, and type: 268, a *colon*, and 421 (4).

At the right side you're able to go from *Portrait* to *Landscape*, and the other way around (5). This means if you typed the numbers in the *wrong order*, you *don't* have to *retype* them; just click on the Landscape or Portrait icon, and the numbers are *reversed* automatically!

Now drag over the girl again. The frame you just drew, now has a *fixed* aspect ratio; a *ratio* of *268* to *421* (6). You can adjust the *size* of the frame (7), but the *aspect ratio* of the frame (*268* to *421*), *will not change*; because it is fixed.

When you drag the frame to the (bottom) edge, it will *snap* to the edge (like a magnet). Press Enter to crop. The image has now been cropped with the *correct aspect ratio*.

Does this mean my image is now 268 *pixels* wide, and 421 *pixels* high? No, not yet. If we look at the top of the screen (8), we see that our image is much *larger*; in my case 1378 pixels wide, and 2068 pixels tall. This *is* the correct *aspect ratio*, but we still have *too many pixels* for placement on the internet. So the next step will be to *reduce* the amount of pixels. *Reducing* the amount of pixels of an image is called *resizing*, and this is the topic of the next lesson.

33. Resizing

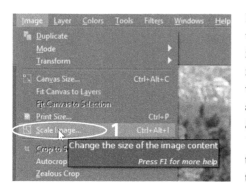

In the previous lesson, we have cropped an image with an aspect ratio of *268:421*. Now we will look at how to *resize* an image. Go to: *Image > Scale Image* (1). Behind *Width* and *Height*, we see the *pixel* dimensions, like they are also shown at the *top* of the *screen* (2). Our image is 1348 pixels wide, and 2118 pixels tall.

I want to reduce the amount of pixels to 268 pixels for the width, and 421 pixels for the height. So in the *Width* entry field, I type 268 (3). When I press *Enter* (4), I see the *Height* is *automatically* updated and recalculated to 421 pixels. This happens because Width and Height are by default *connected*.

To *disconnect* Width and Height, click on the closed *chain*, which then *opens* (5). I want to leave the image *in proportion*, so I will *close* the chain again, by clicking on the open chain.

Quality is by default on *Cubic*, which gives optimal results (6). To scale, click on *Scale*. To see the image at 100%, press *Ctrl-1*. At the top we can see we have the correct size: 268 by 421 pixels (7).

We've looked at how to *crop* and *resize* for the web. Now let's look at how to crop for print. After cropping for print, *we don't have to resize*. For print, the resizing is best done by specialised software on the computer that prepares for the printing, and this will go *automatically*. What we *have* to do though, is to *check* whether our image is *large enough* to print. With large I mean large in the *amount* of *pixels*. Not having *enough* pixels, can make your print look *blurry* (or blocky). It will not print sharp. Let's have a look.

I want to crop for a 4 by 6 inch print. To quickly open one of the ten last opened files, I go to: *File > Open Recent > Girl_crop_original.jpg.*

Select the *Crop* Tool, and in the *Tool Options*, under Fixed, type: 2 : 3 (two colon three), which is the *same* aspect ratio as 4 by 6 (8). Now crop the image.

Next we'll check whether we have *enough* pixels for a sharp print. To make the concept of having *enough* pixels for print *visible*, we will start with using a template. After looking at the template, we will look at how the *Scale Image* window in Gimp gives us the information we need.

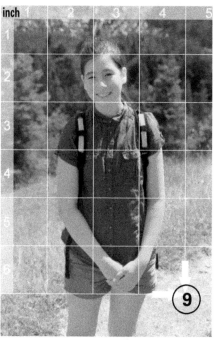

For printing *one inch*, we will have to provide *300 pixels*. 300 pixels in a row, *literally* has a 'length' (in *printing terms)* of 1 inch. This means an image of 150x150 pixels, *isn't* large enough to be printed 1 by 1 inch, but can be printed ½ by ½ inch at its maximum. To print *two* inches, we will need at least *600 pixels*, for 3 inches 900 pixels, etcetera. Open *Pixels_to_inches.xcf.* We will now lay this template *over* the cropped image. Drag the *template* thumbnail on the *image* thumbnail (and down a bit so you see a *plus* sign). Then drag the template into place at the top left (it will snap like a magnet). Press *Ctrl-0* to see the whole image. In the template, each inch has a *length* of 300 pixels. Because our image is *larger* than what the template indicates as to be 4 by 6 inches (9), we can *visually* see we have *enough* pixels.

We don't *need* this template, however, to check for print. It is just a visual demonstration. In Gimp, the *Scale Image* window will give us the information we need. Go to *Image > Scale Image.* Below *Image Size*, there is *resolution*, which is a *print only* area (10). With resolution you *can't* change the amount of pixels. Resolution is just for *calculating* (for checking) whether you have *enough* pixels for print. Select the text behind *X resolution*, type 300 (because 300 is the amount of pixels we need to print 1 inch) and press *Enter* (*Y resolution* is now also 300). Changing the resolution to 300 *didn't* change the *amount* of pixels we have (still 1378 by 2068 pixels).

Now that we have set the correct *resolution* for print (300 pixels per inch), at the right of *Image Size* we have to change *pixels* (px) to *inches* (in) (11).

By changing *pixels* to *inches*, Gimp will now devide 1378 by 300, which is 4,593 (*inch* for the Width), and 2068 by 300, which is 6,893 (*inch* for the Height). Although it's a simple calculation, it is quite helpful for a quick check! We know now what we wanted to know; we have *enough* pixels to print in the size we have in mind (4x6 inch). We know we can print our image *4.5 by 6.8* inches at it's maximum. Printing smaller is always possible. Printing larger isn't.

Since we haven't changed the pixels, when we *close* the Scale Image window, is there a *difference* between choosing *Scale* and *Cancel* (12)? Yes there is. If we choose *Scale*, the *change* we made in *resolution* (setting it to 300) *is saved*. And this is very useful inside of Gimp. Let me show you. I will make the *rulers* visible via: *View > Show Rulers* (rulers are further discussed in lesson 64; making *e-book* covers). At the bottom left, I will set the rulers to *inches* (13).

Now the *rulers* will tell me the *maximum* size I can print my image (14), (and even more precise than the template did that we had opened).

In the next lesson we will look at how to save images for the web.

34. Save images for the web

We have *cropped*, and we have *resized* an image for use on the web.
In this lecture we will look at how to *save* an image for the web.
And in the next lecture we will look at how to save an image for *print*.

Open *Save_for_Web.xcf*.
Then go to: *File > Save for Web* (1).

At the top left we see the three web formats; JPEG, PNG, and GIF (2). So, which one should we choose?

JPEG's are for photographs. With JPEG's it's best to leave *Quality* at 100% or close to 100%. This is because JPEG (or jpg) uses *lossy* compression, which means you can damage your image.

This is what jpg compression looks like if you compress too much. Compression with jpg is a trade-off between *File size* (shown at the bottom), and *image quality*. A *smaller* file size (as a result of *higher* compression) results in *lower* image *quality*. These days with fast internet connections, looking for the lowest file size possible isn't that important anymore.

With Quality at 100% (3), the File size of the image (4) is 114 kB (kB means kiloByte, and 1000 kiloByte is 1 MegaByte or 1 MB).

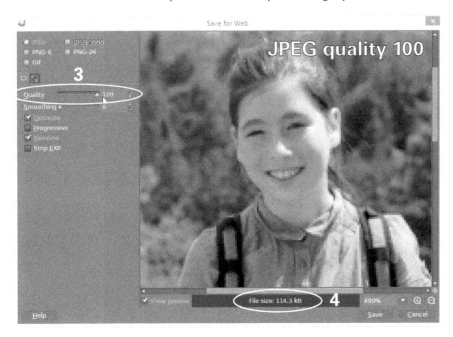

With Quality set at 49%, the File size of the image is only 30 kB, but the image quality really starts to suffer...

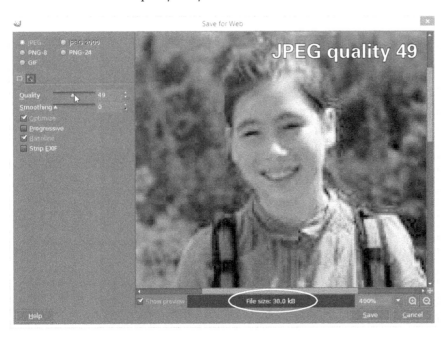

If you click on *Save*, you can give the image a name (5), navigate to a folder, and save the file.

JPEG 2000, or *'jp2'*, is a JPEG variant, (6) but it is not used for the web. It is not supported by web browsers.
You will also need an *extra* plug-in if you want to use jp2.

The next format is PNG. Because PNG uses a *lossless* compression (which means compression *without* losing image quality) PNG is the best choice for saving logo's and icons. PNG comes in two *variations*; PNG-8 and PNG-24. PNG-8 can only show 256 colors, and is from the days of slow internet connections (7). Because of the fast internet connections of today, there is not much use for it anymore.

PNG-24 has normal color, and it supports *high quality transparency*, as we will see in a moment. The File size of this image in the PNG-24 format, is 224 kiloBite

(8). If I choose JPEG, and set *Quality* to 97 (which gives no visible quality loss), we see our File size becomes *much* smaller (79 kB); only a *third* of that of the PNG format (9).

When you use JPEG compression, you can click on *Show preview* (10) to compare the image *with*, and *without* compression, to see whether the quality loss is acceptable or not.

So when do you use PNG?

Where JPEG is the best choice for photographs, PNG-24, is the best choice for logo's and icons. Let's have a look.

Open *Udemy_logo.png*. The Udemy logo has *transparency*, as we can see from the checkerboard pattern. For the internet this means that where is transparency, we are able to look *behind* the logo, which is very powerful. JPEG can't do this, because JPEG *doesn't* support transparency.

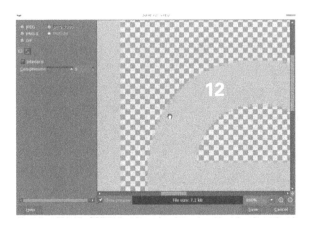

Go to: *File > Save for Web*. As we see, JPEG quickly gives artefacts (11). At *Quality* 85, we can already see the JPEG *compression*. And because JPEG *doesn't* support transparency, the transparent areas are filled in with *white*. The file size of the logo is now 12 kilobyte.

If I switch to PNG, we can see the advantages of PNG.

The *artefacts* in the letters are gone (12), we have *transparency*, and on top of that, we even get a *smaller file size* (7 kB).

The last format is GIF. GIF is also an old web format, and has the *same limitations* as PNG-8. However, GIF has something unique; it can show *animations*.

In the next lesson we will look at how to save for print.

35. Save images for print

If you want a *professional* print of your image, for example printed by
a printing office, or you want to use an image for placement in a magazine,
it's best to save your file in the *tif* file format. Tif stands for: *Tagged Image File
Format*. Tif is sometimes written as *tif*, and sometimes written as *tiff*; both are
the same. Tif is a popular file format in the *graphic design* industry.

To save an image as a *tif*, go to: *File > Export As*. At the top you can give your
file a name. At the bottom left click on *Select File Type* (1). Then scroll to the
bottom. Close to the bottom you will see: *TIFF image* (2). When you click

on it, at the top,
you will see your
file name now ends
with *tif*. Under
Places, navigate
to the folder where
you want to save
the file. Click on

Export, and then click on *Export* again (3).
The file size of a *tif* file, will be *larger* than that of a JPEG or PNG file.

When an image is going to be printed on paper, the *Red*, *Green*, and
Blue color Channels will be translated to a *Cyan*, *Magenta*, *Yellow*,
and *Black* Channel. This conversion is, like the *resizing* of an image
for print, best done by specialized software at the printing office.

When you send your image for print, it is advisable that you include the
term *sRGB* into your file name. So for example: '*Mountains_sRGB.tif*'.
When information about the *sRGB* color space is missing, normally *sRGB* is
automatically assumed. But because there *are more* RGB color spaces, it's
better to include *sRGB* in the file name, so a prepress specialist will know how
to do the conversion correctly.

Gimp *can* do RGB to CMYK conversions, however, this requires *both* an extra
plugin, and *specific* knowledge about color management, which is a relatively
difficult subject. If you're interested in the topic of color management, you can
google for: *Separate+*, which is the *CMYK Separation Plugin* for Gimp.

In the next lesson we will look at transforming layer content.

36. Transformations

In this lecture we will look at four ways to transform the content of a layer; *Scaling*, *Rotating*, *Skewing*, and *Perspective*. Open *Girl_transform.xcf*.

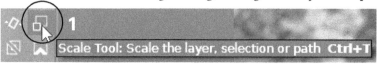

To scale a layer, you can click on the *Scale* tool (1), or you can press *Ctrl-T*. The advantage of pressing *Ctrl-T* is that you can *directly start* scaling. I click Cancel. If you do *not* use the shortcut *Ctrl-T*, and select the *Scale* tool by clicking on it in the *toolbar*, you *first* have to click on the *canvas*, to be able scale.

I scale by dragging a corner. Right now, I'm distorting the proportions (2). To scale *proportionally*, which is what you normally want to do, you have to *hold down* the *Ctrl* key while dragging. To scale, press Enter. I press *Ctrl-Z* to undo.

I click on the *Rotate* tool (3), and click on the canvas. To rotate, drag your mouse (4). You can do this inside or outside the image, this doesn't matter. If you hold down *Ctrl* while you drag, you will rotate in 15 degree increments. So, 15, 30, 45, etc. Press Enter to rotate. I press *Ctrl-Z* to undo.

To skew, click on the *Shear* tool (5), and click on the canvas. To skew, you can drag somewhere inside or outside the image, this doesn't matter (6). Press Enter to skew. Press *Ctrl-Z* to undo.

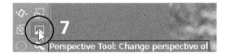

The last transformation tool is the *Perspective* tool (7). Click on it and click on the canvas. If you drag a corner in, you're rotating the image in a *3-dimensional* space (8). Click on *Cancel*.
Let's place the image on a computer screen.

Open *Screen.jpg*. Here we have a laptop screen that's placed in perspective. The laptop screen has an aspect ratio of 16 by 10 (*16:10*, or *8:5*). So I need to *crop* my image in the *correct dimensions* first.

Select *Fixed*, and below, type: 16:10 (9). Now crop the image (10), and drag the cropped image over.

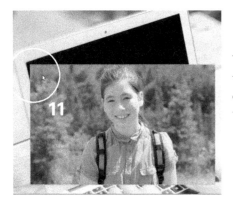

With the *Move* tool, position the top left corner of the image, close to the top left corner of the laptop screen (11).

To *only* see the *changes* that you make with the Transform tool, *hide* the *layer* by dragging *Opacity* to 0% (12).

Now select the *Perspective* tool, and click on the canvas.

To see the *preview* image of the Transform tool, in the *Tool Options*, *Show image preview* must be selected. Below I set the *Opacity* of the preview image to 100% (13), because I like to see the image *without* transparency when I do a transformation.

Now I first drag each corner approximately into place (14, 15).

Then I zoom in (to about 300%), and *fine-tune* the placement of the corners (16).

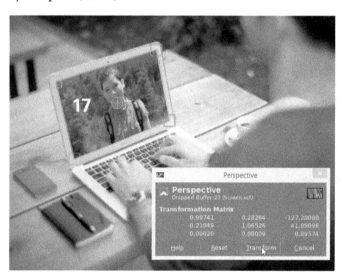

I press Enter to transform. I set the *Opacity* of the *layer* back to 100%.

The image has been placed in perspective on the laptop screen (17).

With the transformation tools, you can not only transform *layers*. You can also transform *selections* and *paths* with the four transformation tools. Let's look at an important difference between transforming *selections* and *paths*.

Open *Selection_vs_path.xcf*. On top, we have a text layer (17). The use of text is explored further in the next lesson. There are *three* ways to make the text (the letter a) larger. We can enlarge the letter a just as normal *text*, as a *selection*, and as a *path*.

In order to compare transforming *selections* and *paths*, I will first enlarge the letter a as a *selection*, and then enlarge the letter a as a *path*.

Make a *selection* from the letter a by *Alt-clicking* on the text layer. Then select the *Scale* tool (19). To scale a *selection*, in the *Tool Options*, behind *Transform*, click on the *Selection* icon (20).

Now click on the canvas. Press *Ctrl* to constrain the proportions, and drag a corner out. Click on *Scale*. Select the *Move* tool, and *Alt*-drag the selection a bit to the right. *Shift*-click on the *New layer* icon, and press *Alt-Backspace* to fill the selection with black.

Press *Ctrl-D* to deselect. As we can see, the enlarged a looks blurry (21). The reason for this, is that *selections* are *pixel-based*. The solution for this, is to scale *not* as a selection, but as a *path*.

To do this, *right*-click on the text layer, and choose: *Text to Path* (22). Gimp has now made a *path* of the letter a. Click on the *Paths* panel. We see a path that has been called 'a' (22). If you make the eye of the path visible (23), on the canvas you will see a *red outline* of the path. Go to the *Layers* panel, and make a new layer.

Now select the *Scale* tool. In the *Tool Options*, behind Transform, select the *Path* icon (24).

Now click on the canvas. Zoom out (for example to 12%). Press *Ctrl* to constrain the proportions, and drag the corners out. You can move the frame around while you're scaling, by dragging the frame in the center, inside the *circle* with the cross (25). In the next lesson I will demonstrate an *easier* (and more precise!) way to scale a path, with which you *don't* have to zoom out.

26 **27** Selection Path

Click on *Scale* (26). In the *Paths* panel, *Alt*-click on the thumbnail to get a selection from it. Click on the eye to *hide* the *red outline* of the path again (27). Go to the *Layers* panel, and fill the selection with black by pressing *Alt-Backspace*. We can now see the path gives a very sharp result (28). This is because a path is resolution (and thus pixel) *independent*. No matter the size, a path will *always* be sharp. This is the reason why logos are normally made in a 'vector' program like Inkscape, where you work only with paths. Inkscape is like Illustrator, and is Open Source.

Now let's have a look at the *Rectangle* layer. Hide all the 'a' layers, and make the *Rectangle* layer visible (29). Let's say we want to make the black rectangle much *higher*. I *Alt*-click on the *Rectangle* layer to get a selection of its shape. Then, in the *Tool Options*, click on the *Selection* icon, in order to scale a *selection* with the Scale tool. Click on the canvas, and drag the bottom down (29). Click on *Scale*. Create a new layer, and fill the selection with black. Press *Ctrl-D* to deselect, and hide the original *Rectangle* layer.

We can see that the *top* and *bottom* (that have been scaled up) have become *blurry* (30). The solution for this could be converting to a path again, but there is an easier way.

31

32

Alt-click on the *Rectangle* layer again. As we saw in lesson 22 (The Rectangle and Ellipse select tool), we can make a normal *rectangle* or *ellipse* selection *adjustable again* by clicking on it. So to make our rectangle selection *adjustable* again for use with the *Rectangle* select tool, just click on it *with* the *Rectangle* select tool.

Now I will drag the bottom down again, just like I did with the *Scale* tool (31). I make a new layer, and fill the selection with black. I press *Ctrl-D* to deselect (32).
As we can see, *scaling* a normal rectangular selection *up*, with the *Rectangle* select tool, *doesn't* give a blurry result, and works fast.

When the selection is more complex than just a simple rectangle or ellipse, you *do* need to convert to a path before scaling (when the result has to remain sharp). But when the selection comes from a layer *mask* (to do this: *right-click* on the *mask > Mask to Selection*) and the *mask* also contains *soft* edges (which normally is the case), you must *scale* as a *selection*, in order to keep the *softness* of the edges.

You can also *flip*, or, *mirror* a layer. To do this, go to: *Layer > Transform > Flip Horizontally* (33, 34).
Flipping *Vertically* is the same as flipping *Horizontally*, followed by a 180 degree *rotation*.

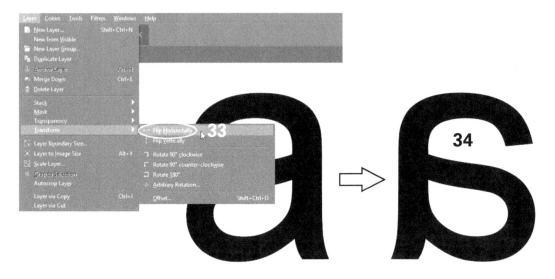

If you have an image that's not scanned straight, or you have a picture of a landscape with a skewed horizon, you can use the *Measure* tool to straighten your image. Open *Beach.jpg*. Go to: *Tools > Measure* (35). I draw a line across the horizon. I can zoom in and adjust the end

points (36) if needed. At the bottom, I can see that the *angle* of the line (from left to right) is *1,37* degrees (37).

This means the horizon of the image is slightly *pointing upwards*. So to make the horizon horizontal, we have to *rotate* our image 1,37 degrees *clockwise*. I select the *Rotate* tool and click on the canvas. Behind *Angle* I will type: 1,37 (you have to use a *comma* instead of a period for the decimal point). Then press *Enter to apply the numeric value*. After having pressed Enter, click on *Rotate* (38).

I will remove the transparent edges with the *Crop* tool (39).

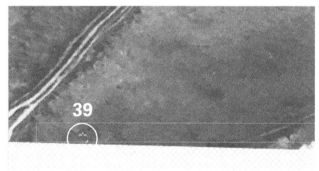

Finally, we will look at the difference between rotating a single *layer*, versus rotating the entire *image*. Open *Canyon_portrait.jpg*. I would like to change this image from *landscape* to *portrait*. To do this, I need to rotate the *image*, and *not* the layer. Let's see what happens if I would rotate the *layer*. Then I would go to: *Layer > Transform > Rotate 90 clockwise* (40).

I have now rotated the *layer*, but *not* the *image*. I press *Ctrl-Z* to undo (41).

To rotate the whole *image*, I must use the *Image* menu (not the *Layer* menu). I go to: *Image > Transform > Rotate 90 clockwise* (42).

Now I have rotated the *image*, from landscape to portrait (43).

In the next lesson we will look at using text.

37. Using text

In this lecture we will look at the *Text* tool.
You can click on the *Text* tool in the *toolbar*,
or you can press *T* (1). Now drag a frame
on the canvas.

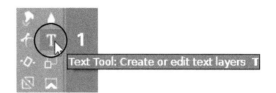

As with the *Rectangle* select tool, you can adjust the *size* of the frame
by dragging the sides and the corners (2). The text frame is the
container or boundary for the text. The text cannot go outside this
frame. This is the way how *Desktop Publishing* programs work.

I will type Gimp (3). The default text color will be the
Foreground color. To change the text color, go to the

Tool Options, and click behind
Color on the colored thumbnail
(4). I will change the color of the
text to a grey, by dragging *Value*
to about 60 (5), and press Enter. To continue typing,
click inside the text frame, to select the frame again.
Now I type a space, and the word text.

If you hold down the *Alt*-key,
the *Move* tool icon will appear
(6). So by pressing *Alt*, you can
move the frame around, by
dragging inside the frame.

To change the text size, in the *Tool Options* click behind *Size*
in the text entry field, so
you get a blinking cursor
(7).

With the *up* and *down*
arrow keys, it's now easy to
adjust the text size. If you
keep an arrow key pressed
down longer, you go faster.

If you want to change the *size* of an *individual* letter, for example you want to make the *G* bigger, use the *small menu* above the text. Select the *G* by dragging over it (8). In the small menu, click inside the *text size* entry field, to get a blinking cursor (9). With your up and down arrow keys, adjust the size of the *G*. Click somewhere in the text box to deselect the *G*. If you now go to the *Tool Options*, you will see that changing the text size from *here*, doesn't affect the *G* anymore. The *G* now can *only* be adjusted with the small menu. If you want the *G* to be a normal letter again, select it, and click on the *Clear style of selected text* icon at the left (10). You can now adjust the *G* again with the *Tool Options*.

To explore the text options further, let's insert some placeholder text. Double-click on *Lorem ipsum.txt* to open it (11). Copy the text by pressing *Ctrl-A* to select all the text, and then *Ctrl-C* to copy the text. Go to Gimp, and click inside the text frame. To delete the text in the text frame press *Ctrl-A*, and then press *Backspace*. Paste the copied text by pressing *Ctrl-V*. As we can see, there is too much text to fit the frame (12). Let's make the text smaller, and set the size to 20. If you want the text *frame* to be less wide, you can drag the *left or right* side of the text frame in (13). At the bottom you can see the *dimensions* of the text frame (14). I'll drag the *width* of the frame to about 400 pixels (15).

In the *Tool Options* you can align the text. At the right of *Justify* you can choose: *Left* (standard), *Right* (16), *Centered* (17), and *Filled* (18).

Below *Justify*, you can *indent* the first line of a *new paragraph*. Click in the text entry field, and with your up and down arrow keys you can adjust the distance (19, 20). Below is *line spacing* (21). You can increase or decrease the line spacing (22). Below line spacing is *letter spacing* (23); here you can adjust the space *between* the letters (24).

To select a word, you *double-click* on it (25). To select a paragraph, you *triple* click (26). And to select all text in the frame, press *Ctrl-A* (27). Click in the text to deselect.

To break up a word at the end of a sentence, type a *hyphen* inside that word.

To choose a different font, in the *Tool Options* click on the white font icon (28). You get a list where you can see your fonts. You can quickly scroll through the list by using the scroll bar at the right (29).

You can make the font previews larger and smaller by clicking on the plus and minus magnifying glasses (30).

You can *search* a font by *name*. To do this, select the text under *Font*. Let's say I want to use Arial. If I type the first letter, the letter a (31) (and this *doesn't* have to be a capital letter) I see all fonts that start with an a (32). I can scroll through them.

If I type a second letter, the letter r (33), the list gets *smaller* and shows all fonts that start with ar (34).

I also type i and a (35), and the Arial font-family remains (36). I have five different font-weights to choose from: Regular, Bold, Bold-italic, Heavy, and Italic.

To experiment with some different fonts, it's convenient to use the *Fonts* panel (37). Click on a font, and by pressing the *up* and *down* arrow keys, you can directly preview new fonts. Holding the up or down arrow key pressed down, let's you go through the list *fast*.

If you don't have the Text *tool* selected, and you're not working on a text *layer*, *double-clicking* on a text *layer* will automatically select the Text *tool* for you! Click inside the text frame and you can type.

You can also *kern* text. *Kerning* is adjusting the space between *two individual letters*. This way, you can position *each letter* exactly where you want. Kerning is used for important and usually *larger* text. For example to make the title of a book cover, or the name of a logo, look more professional or unique. I delete all text in the frame, and type Perfect match as a title. I make the text frame a bit larger, to about 700 pixels wide. In the *Tool Options* I set the letter spacing back to 0. I click inside the *Font size* text entry field, and set the size to about 120.

To improve the text, I think I want to reduce the distance between the P and the e a bit. To do this, I place the cursor between the P and the e (38). In the panel above, at the bottom right, is the *Change kerning* entry field. I click inside the entry field, to get a blinking cursor.

Now I use the up and down arrow keys, to adjust the distance. I think -6 looks good (39).

Because individual letters that are adjusted with the *small* panel (above the text frame), become *unresponsive* to changes in the *Tool Options* panel, and can't be resized anymore via the *Tool Options*, it's best to save specially *kerned* text that you've been working on, as a *path*. This has several advantages. First, you can *scale, rotate, skew, and* place the text in *perspective* (3-dimensionally), *all* without losing *any* sharpness of the text, which is very powerful. Second, you can also *save* the path of the kerned text. When you save a path, you can open the saved path and use it in *other* documents. Let's see how this works. First *right-click* on the text layer, and choose: *Text to Path* (40).

In the *Paths* panel, I now have a path of the *kerned* text (41). To *save* the path, I go to: *Configure this tab > Paths Menu > Export Path* (42).

You can save the path where you want. I will create a *folder* in the .gimp-2.8 folder, named: *Paths*, to keep my paths all in one place, so I don't have to search for them.

I call the path `Perfect match`, and click on *Save* (43).

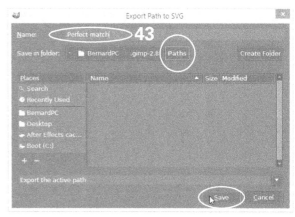

To *open* your path in another file, go to the *Paths* panel. Go to: *Configure this tab > Paths Menu > Import Path.*

At the bottom right, click on *Scalable SVG image*, and choose: *All files* (44). Now select the path you saved (45).

Selecting *Scale imported paths to fit image* is very helpful when the pixel dimensions of your *current* file differs greatly from the one the path was *originally* made in (46). Click on *Open*.

We have now *imported* a path. To see the path as a red outline, make the eye of the path visible. To scale the path with *ease* and *precision*, first *Alt*-click on the path thumbnail to get a *selection* of the path. Now select the *Scale* tool. In the *Tool Options*, make sure the *Path icon* is selected. Then click on the canvas.

To scale the path proportionally, press *Ctrl* and drag a corner (or side). You can also *move* the path, by dragging the circle in the middle (47). Then click on *Scale*.

Alt-click on the path thumbnail again, to get a *new* selection (now from the adjusted path). Create a new layer, *fill* the selection, an deselect (48).

In the next lesson we will look at how to insert special characters, called 'glyphs'.

38. Using Glyphs

Most fonts have special characters, often referred to as glyphs. In this lecture we will install a glyphs file, which will serve as a glyphs panel. With the file, you can quickly find a *special* character. Download the file that comes with this lecture, called *Glyphs.xcf*. I will place this file in the .gimp-2.8 folder for quick access.

In the .gimp-2.8 folder, I will create a new folder called *Glyphs*, and place the *Glyphs.xcf* file in the *Glyphs* folder. In Gimp I go to *File > Open*. I navigate to the *Glyphs* folder in the .gimp-2.8 folder, and *bookmark* the *Glyphs* folder. The glyphs file can now be accessed quickly.

Open *Arrow.xcf*. It has a text layer with the text Arrow. If you *double*-click on the text layer, the *Text* tool will be selected *automatically*! The font used here is Times New Roman. Let's say I need a special character for the o.

Go to: *File > open*, or press *Ctrl-O*. Click on *Glyphs*, and click on *Open*. To quickly zoom in and make the *Glyphs* document *fill* the window (from *side* to *side*), go to: *View > Zoom > Fill Window* (1).

With the scrollbar at the right, you can quickly scroll through the list of glyphs.

At the top, we have the small and capital letters with diacritical marks. Let's say I need an o with a circumflex. I drag over the glyph (2), and press: *Ctrl-C*. I go back to my Arrow document, drag over the o (3), and press: *Ctrl-V* (4).

Let's also place a *bullet* point. I click on the Glyphs document, and scroll to the bottom. I drag over the small bullet (5). I *right-* click, and choose: *Copy* (6).

I go back to my Arrow document, and click in front of the A (7). I *right*-click, and choose: *Paste* (8). If you want a larger bullet, you can choose the larger bullet at the right of the small bullet (9). And if you want a square bullet, you can choose the square at the left (10).

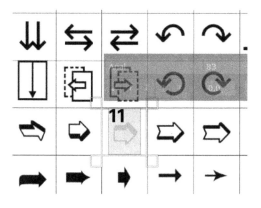

Finally, let's insert an arrow. Scroll to the arrow section. Select an arrow and copy it (11). Go back, click behind the W, and paste the arrow (12).

In the next lecture we will look at Blending modes.

39. Blending modes (1)

In the lecture about selecting hair, we have already seen a blending mode in action. Blending modes are different ways to *interact* with the layers below. With a blending mode you *don't* have to lower the *opacity* of the layer to see through the *content*. Some blending modes *darken* the underlaying layers (with the *content* of the layer, that uses the blending mode), and some *lighten up* the underlaying layers. There are also blending modes that make underlying layers darker *and* lighter at the same time, increasing *contrast*. Open *Mountains.jpg*. If you click at the right side of *Mode* (1), you see the list of the blending modes. They are placed in *groups*. On top (*Lighten only*, *Screen*, *Dodge*, and *Addition*) is the *lighten* group (2). These Blending modes make the underlaying layers lighter, in different ways. Below is the *darken* group (*Darken only*, *Multiply*, *Burn*) (3). They make the underlaying layers darker. Then we have the *contrast* groups (4), and on the bottom (*Hue*, *Saturation*, *Color*, and *Value*) we have the *color* blending modes (5).
The *color* blending modes are discussed in the next lesson.

Blending modes give you results that are not possible to get in another way. To see a blending mode in action, you need *two* layers or more. The blending mode will be applied to the *top* layer. The layer or layer's under it, are the ones that the top layer will interact with. Open *Stars.jpg* and *Mountains.jpg*. The *Stars* image has stars in the sky. I would like to borrow the stars from the *Stars* image and *place* them in the sky of the *Mountains* image. Drag the *Stars* image over to the *Mountains* image (6). Go to *Mode*, and choose the *Lighten only* blending mode (7). Now we have stars in the sky (8).

So how does *Lighten only* work? What the *Lighten only* blending mode does is it makes a *comparison*: which layer has the *lightest color*? Is it the layer with the blending mode, or any of the layers below it? For each pixel, this comparison is made. The lightest pixel wins, and will be shown.

I just want the stars, and not the light mountains that have become visible at the bottom (9). So I will *remove* the light mountains using a layer *mask*. *Right*-click on the top layer and choose *Add Layer mask*. Choose a white mask, and press Enter. To hide the mountains, paint with black. Press *B* to select the brush, and in the *Tool Options* choose a hard brush. Increase the size to about 400. After painting away the light mountains *only* the stars will now come through (10). You can lower the *Opacity* of the *Stars* layer a bit to get a more subtle effect.

Next we'll look at the *opposite* of *Lighten only*: *Darken only*. We've already seen this blending mode in action in lesson 31 about selecting hair. Let's explore *Darken only* a bit further. Open *Amsterdam.jpg*, *Clouds.jpg*, and *Birds.jpg*.
I would like to place some clouds in the sky. Drag the *Clouds* image over to the *Amsterdam* image (11). Go to *Mode*, and choose *Darken only* (12).

With *Darken only*, only the *darkest* pixels will be shown. That's why we see the clouds; the Clouds are *darker* than the very bright sky (13). Below the sky, we see the buildings, because the buildings are *darker* than the clouds.

Let's optimize the result a bit. To prevent that the clouds will interact with the buildings, I make a selection of the cloudless sky in the Amsterdam layer. To do this, click in the *lightest* area of the sky with the *Fuzzy* select tool, and drag the *Threshold* to about 120 (14).

With the selection loaded, *right*-click on the *Clouds* layer, and choose: *Add Layer Mask*. Click on *Selection*, and press Enter. Press *Ctrl-D* to deselect. I still see a bit of *white* from the *old* sky inside some trees (15). To *reveal* the

new sky in the trees, press *B* to select the brush and set the size to about 60. Paint with *white* in the layer *mask* to reveal the new sky.

What I would like to do is to create a *new* layer from what I see now, like a *snapshot*. To do this, *right*-click on the top layer, and choose: *New from visible* (16). I have now added a *flattened* version of my document, in *one* layer.

I will now *brighten* this new layer. Press *Ctrl-L* to open *Levels*, and drag the middle slider to the left.

I also would like to put some birds in the sky. Open *Birds.jpg*. Drag the birds over (17).
I want to see the birds, but *hide* it's background to see the clouds underneath. I will start by setting the birds layer to *Darken only* (18).

Because almost *everything* on the Birds layer is *darker* than the sky underneath, almost the complete *Birds* layer stays visible (19).

To change this, I will open *Levels*. I will brighten the image with the midtone slider, until the background of the birds gets *lighter* than the sky under it (20).

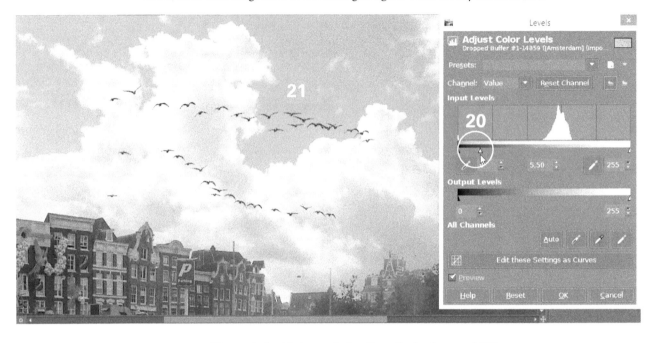

Now *only* the birds are darker than the background (21).

Next we will look at *Screen* and *Multiply*. Like *Lighten only* and *Darken only*, *Screen* and *Multiply* are *opposites*.
Open *Mountains.jpg* and *Girl_crop.jpg*. Drag the girl image over. I place the girl layer partially over the dark mountains. When I set the girl layer on *Lighten only*, I will see only the *lightest* pixels (22). This means only *part* of the girl, and only a *part* of the Mountains. But what if I want to see both images completely? Below *Lighten only*, select *Screen*.
Screen can be compared to using *two separate slide projectors*, who are both projecting on the *same* screen. One projector shows the mountains, the other projector shows the girl. Where the two images overlap, we get a *slightly lighter* result, but *both* images *will* be visible, which is what we want.

Open *Lens_flare.jpg*. I would like to *add* this lens flare to the girl image, to give it a sunny effect. I drag it over.

For adding the stars, we used *Lighten only*. If we use *Lighten only* for the lens flare however, we're not getting the result we are looking for. There is no real blending going on (23). The only way to add the *actual light* from the flare, is to use the double slide projector technique provided by *Screen* mode (24).

Screen can also be used to lighten an image *itself*. I hide the flare, and make a duplicate of the girl layer (25). I set the duplicate on *Screen* (26).

With *Opacity* I can adjust the amount of light coming from the 'second projector' (27).

You can also *colorize* an image with *Screen*, to bring a certain mood to an image. To warm the image up, I could fill a new layer with orange. Then I set the layer to *Screen*, and drag the *Opacity* down (to about 10 percent). With *Hue-Saturation* I could adjust the *tint* of the orange (by using the Hue slider), to try different results.

You can also *paint* with colored light, using a soft brush. You could make different layers, each layer having a specific color. When you give these layers a black layer *mask*, you can *add* and *remove* colored light from each layer. When you set the brush opacity low (10%), you can gradually add and remove light. Press *X*, to alternate between painting with black and white.

The *opposite* of *Screen* is *Multiply*. For *Screen*, we had the comparison of having *two* projectors, each showing an image. With *Multiply* we're back to *one* projector, showing *both* images at the *same time*. You can compare it to a *light table*, where you lay two transparent sheets on top of each other. The second sheet will make the result *darker*. Open *Rails.jpg*.

Let's say I want an orange circle, and I want to be able to see the background *through* the orange circle. For this, we'll need the *light table* effect. Create a new layer. To draw a circle, select the *Ellipse* select tool. Start dragging, and then add the *Shift* key. To position the circle, drag in the middle of the circle. Now open the color panel, and select an orange (for example: 255, 90, 0). On an empty layer, fill the selection by pressing *Alt-Backspace*. Press *Ctrl-D* to deselect. Now choose *Multiply* (28). I lower the *Opacity* just a bit (to 90%), to get a nice orange.

Below *Multiply* we have *Burn*. Open *Building.xcf*. *Burn* is a variation of *Multiply*, and gives a more dramatic effect. It brings more contrast and saturation, providing a *cinematic* look.

The next group is the *contrast* group. Open *Plaster.xcf*. Let's say I want to mix the plaster and the underlying image. With *Screen* (the two projector method) the result becomes too *light*. And with *Multiply* (the light table method) the result becomes too *dark*. The solution for this is *Overlay*. *Overlay* is a *combination* of Screen and Multiply. *Overlay* will make the light tones lighter, and the dark tones darker, increasing *contrast*. A more extreme version of *Overlay* is *Hard light*. Like we saw with *Burn*; *Hard light* gives more *contrast* and more *saturation*.

You can also *combine* blending modes. Set the *wrinkled paper* layer to *Overlay*. To make the effect *stronger*, I duplicate the layer. Now the result is getting too *light*. The solution is to change the top layer to *Multiply* (29), to get the desired result. You can lower the *Opacity* to reduce the strength. We now have *Overlay* and *Multiply* working *together*.

Difference shows the *difference* between two layers. This is very helpful with *aligning* images. Open *Align_1.jpg* and *Align_2.jpg*. Drag *Align_2* over. I could align the two layers by lowering the *Opacity* of the top layer. However, it will be quite difficult to see. If I choose *Difference*, it becomes easier to see. Black means perfectly aligned. Light colors indicate difference. Now it's much easier to see what's aligned and what is not.

In the next chapter we will see *Grain extract* and *Grain merge* in action. They are the basis of a professional skin retouching technique called *frequency separation*.
In the next lesson we will look at the *Color* blending modes.

40. Blending modes (2)

The Color blending modes are: *Hue*, *Saturation*, *Color*, and *Value*. *Color* is the combination of *Hue* and *Saturation*.
The *Hue* blending mode is often used when a *Value* adjustment (with *Levels* or *Curves*) comes with an undesired side effect concerning the color.
Open *Canyon.jpg*. Open *Levels*. The more you make the midtones darker, the more you can see the *orange* sand is shifting to *red* sand. If you only want the sand to be darker, and *not* also to become more red, you use the *Hue* blending mode. Before using *Levels*, first duplicate the layer. Set the blending mode of the top layer to *Hue* (1). This layer will now function as a filter, and will *only* let the *Value* changes come through. Click on the bottom layer, and open *Levels*. If you now make the midtones darker, you will see *no* color change. Click on *OK*. If you hide the blending mode layer, you can see the difference between using the Hue 'filter', and without using this filter.

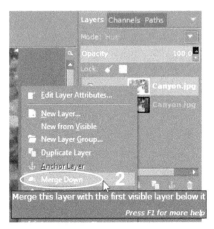

If you want to, you can *merge* the two layers *together* (making them a *single* layer). You do this by *right*-clicking on the top layer, and choose *Merge Down* (2, 3).
Undo the merging by pressing *Ctrl-Z*.

You can also keep the layers separated, and put them in a *folder*.
Click on the *Create a new layer group* icon (4, 5).

Drag the layers in the *Layer Group* folder (6, 7, 8).

You can close the folder by clicking on the *triangle* in front of the folder (9). Now it is just like having *one* layer.

When you *select* the Layer Group *thumbnail*, you can *move* and even *scale* the Layer Group, as it is *one* layer. If you *scale* the Layer Group, *all* layers that are inside the Layer group scale with it (10)!

You can *also* adjust each layer inside the Layer Group *individually*.

Now let's look at *Color*. Open *Girl_crop.jpg*. Create a new empty layer and set it on *Color*. Open the color window, and choose pure green (0,255,0).

Select the brush. Where you paint over the blue shirt (11, 12) the shirt will now become green. The *Value* of the bottom layer will come through. *Hue* (and *Saturation*) come from the *top* layer. Because the buttons of the shirt also have become green now, you can hide them again by using a layer *mask* for the top layer. Paint with black over the buttons, inside the *mask*.

The last blending mode is *Value*. Open *Color_cast.jpg*. Open the *Channels* panel. We can see that the *Red* channel is *lighter* than the *Green* and *Blue* channels (13). This is the main reason for the red color cast. So making the Red channel *darker*, will remove the red color cast.

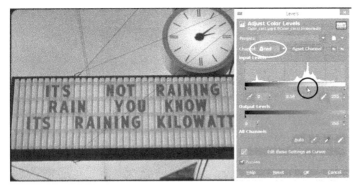

Open *Levels*. Go to the *Red* channel, and make it darker.

Although we have lost the color cast, we *also* made the image *darker*. If you want to do a color correction, *without* colors becoming lighter or darker, use the *Value* blending mode.

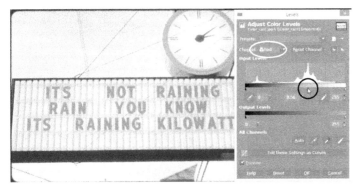

Go to the *Layers* panel and duplicate the layer. Set the blending mode to *Value*. Select the bottom layer. Open *Levels* and go to the *Red* channel again. If you now drag the slider, you see you're losing the red, but the image *doesn't* become darker.

In the next lesson we will look at methods for blurring.

41. Methods for blurring

Blurring is used for many things. It can be used to create depth of field, for retouching, vignetting, text effects, and for creating drop shadows.

Alternative ways for blurring are motion blur and Bokeh, which will be discussed in the *Nik collection* chapter, as well as vignette blurring. Blurring for skin retouching (1), called *frequency separation*, is discussed in the Retouching chapter.

In this lesson we will create a drop shadow, a glow, a text fading effect, and depth of field. We will also look at the *Smudge* tool, with which you can smear pixels like wet paint.

We'll start making a drop shadow. Create a new document, and make it 600 by 300 pixels. Click on the Foreground color, and make a grey by dragging *Value* to about 75. Then click on the Background color, and make a lighter grey. Click on OK. Fill the layer with the Foreground color by pressing *Alt-Backspace* (2).

Create a new layer, and call it paper (3). Press *M* to select the *Rectangle* tool. Drag a rectangle, and press *Ctrl-Backspace* to fill it with the Background color (4). Press *Ctrl-D* to deselect.

Create a new layer for the shadow, and drag it below the paper layer. Call it shadow (5).

Alt-click on the paper layer to get a selection from it. Click with the *Rectangle* tool *inside* the selection, to make it adjustable. Drag the sides a bit in (6).

Go to *Paths*, and click on the *Selection to Path* thumbnail (7). Press *Ctrl-D* to deselect, and double-click on the path thumbnail. Press *Ctrl*, and *add* a point in the middle at the bottom. Drag the added point up a bit (8). You can also use your *arrow* keys, to move the point.

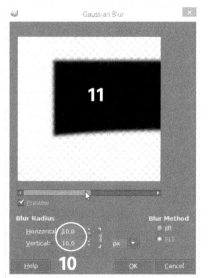

Alt-click on the path *thumbnail* to get a selection, and press *V* to select the *Move* tool. Press *D* to set the Foreground to black, and, with the shadow layer selected, press *Alt-Backspace* to fill the selection with black. Press *Ctrl-D* to deselect. Drag the shadow down a bit (9).

Now we will blur the shadow. Go to: *Filters > Blur > Gaussian Blur*. Set Blur *Radius* to 10 pixels, by scrolling in the text entry field (10). In the Preview window you can see the result (11). Click on OK.

Select the *Move* tool, and click once on the canvas. Now with your arrow keys, you can fine-tune the position of the shadow (12).

You can drag the *Opacity* of the shadow layer down a bit (13).

Now we'll make a glow. Press *D* to set the Fore- and Background to black and white. Open the Color window, and make a light blue (14). Click on OK. *Shift*-click on the new layer icon. Drag the Foreground color on the canvas. Press *X* to switch the Fore- and Background color. Open the *Glyphs* panel, by going to: *File > Open > Glyphs*. Click on

Open. Zoom in a bit and look for the cloud with the sun behind it. Press *T* to select the *Text* tool. Drag over the icon, *right*-click, and choose *Copy* (15). Go to the glow document, click on the canvas, and press *Ctrl-V*. In the *Tool Options*, click on the text *Color* square, select white, and click on OK. Click in the *Font size* text entry field. Hold the arrow up key pressed down until size 300. Press *Alt* and drag *inside* the text frame (16)

to position the cloud. In the *Tool Options*, click on the text *Color* square again, to open the *Text Color* window. In this window, click on the *eyedropper* at the right, and click in the image on the *blue*, to make the cloud also blue (now everything is blue). Click on OK. Select the blue layer, and *Shift*-click on the new layer icon. *Alt*-click on the text layer to get a selection from it. Go to: *Select > Grow*. I will grow my selection with 20 pixels (17). Click on OK (18).

Drag the Foreground color on the canvas (as an alternative for *Alt-Backspace*) (19). Press *Ctrl-D* to deselect.

Because we have just used Gaussian Blur, you can go to: *Filters > Re-Show "Gaussian Blur"* (20). For *Blur Radius* set 30 pixels. Click on OK (21).

We can also use Gaussian Blur in just *one direction* (horizontal or vertical), for example to give text a *faded effect*. Open *The man on the train.xcf*. Press *Ctrl-1* to get a 100% view. Duplicate the text layer twice. Select the middle text layer. Go to: *Filters > Re-Show "Gaussian Blur"*. I only want to blur horizontally.

To do this, click on the *chain* icon, to *disconnect* equal blurring (22).

Set *Vertical* to zero (23). For Horizontal, let's try 400. Click on OK (24).

Next select the *bottom* text layer. Go to: *Filters > Re-Show "Gaussian Blur"*. Set Horizontal blur to 20 pixels (25). Click on OK (26).
Now the text has a bit of extra glow to it. You can adjust the strength of the glow by lowering the *Opacity*.

We will look at more effects for text in the *Google Nik collection* chapter.

Now let's look at *depth of field*, which is another use of blur. Open *Wood.jpg*. I would like to create some depth of field at the right, to direct the viewers eye to the left. Select the *Blur / Sharpen* tool (27). In the *Tool Options*, by default, *Blur* is selected (28). If you click on *Sharpen*, the tool will do the *opposite* of blurring: it will sharpen.

Rate determines the *strength* of the blurring or sharpening (29). I set it to 100%.

I will work with a large, soft brush. I set the size to about 800, so the brush *covers* the area I want to adjust.

I drag a couple of times from the top to the bottom. Now we see the sharpness slowly fades at the right, introducing a bit *depth* to the image.

At the left of the *Blur / Sharpen* tool, we have the *Smudge* tool (30).

With the *Smudge* tool you can smear pixels like wet paint (31).

Open *Old_man.xcf*. I used the *Smudge* tool here, to create a painted effect (32). Different brushes with the Smudge tool give different results.

To prepare for getting a painted effect with the *Smudge* tool, I first *sharpened* the image quite a bit, to get strong contours. To do this, go to: *Filters > Enhance > Unsharp mask*. Drag the window out to get a bigger preview.
What *Unsharp Mask* does, is it is looking at the *edges* in an image, and it will increase the *contrast of these edges*. With *Radius* (33) you set how *many* pixels, at the *left* and *right* side of an edge, are given more contrast (33). So you determine the *width* of the edge, that is given more contrast. This means that if you want to sharpen the *finer detail* in an image, you have to set the *Radius* smaller, and if you if you want to sharpen the *larger details*, you have to set the *Radius* larger.

With *Amount* (35) you determine *how strong* the contrast will be. Dragging the slider to the right will *increase* the contrast (36).

Threshold (37) protects edges with lower contrast, so it *excludes areas* with *less contrast* from being sharpened. The higher the *Threshold*, the more edges that are *not* being sharpened.

For my paint effect, I will increase the *Radius* to 6,3, which will amplify the *larger details* and *lines* of the face. I set *Amount* to 1,5.

Now select the *Smudge* tool. To create a *paint* effect, I will use a brush with fine detail. I select *Grass* (38).

For the *Smudge* tool it is important, that the *Spacing* is set to 1. In the *Brushes panel* at the bottom, I drag the *Spacing* slider to the left (39).

In the *Tool Options*, *Rate* determines how *far* the pixels can be *dragged out*, or how 'wet' the paint is (40).

When I set *Rate* at 99% (100% is *infinite* repetition), I can drag pixels *further* out, than when *Rate* is set lower, for example at 70%. I will set *Rate* to 70% for the paint effect.

I will use a soft brush. I zoom in to 300%, and set the brush size to 20. With the *Grass* brush, I paint in the same direction that the lines are going.

In the next lesson we will look at how to make gradients.

42. Making gradients

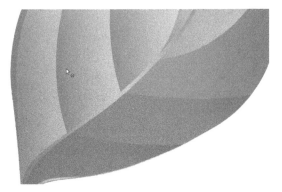

A gradient is a color *transition* from one color to another color. To create a gradient, select the *Blend* tool (1). If you now drag over the canvas, you'll see a *line* with a begin point and an end point (2). The *begin* point is the Foreground color, the *end* point is the Background color. The line

between these points will be the *transition area* between the Fore- and Background color.

You can drag in any direction, and you can drag a longer or shorter gradient. To draw a perfect *horizontal* or *vertical* line, press *Ctrl* while dragging. A gradient is also an efficient way to *blend two images*. *Right*-click on the top layer, and choose: *Add Layer Mask*. I choose *White*, and press Enter. I blend the images by dragging a black and white gradient inside the layer *mask* (3).

Now let's make a colored gradient. Click on the Foreground color to open the Color window and choose yellow. Then click on the Background color, and choose red. Click on OK. We can now make a gradient going from yellow to red.

In the *Tool Options* we can change the *Shape* of the gradient. By default we have a *Linear* gradient. Click on *Linear* (4), and choose *Radial* (5). With *Radial*, the Foreground color becomes the *center*.

Above *Shape* we see a *thumbnail* of the colors we're currently using (6). By default these are the Fore- and Background color (now going from yellow to red). When I click on the thumbnail, I get a list with options. I see I am able to make a gradient from the Foreground (FG) to *transparency* (7).

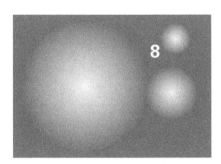

This means I can now add yellow spheres, *without* removing the rest of the image (8).

I set *Radial* back to *Linear*.

Below Foreground to transparency, there are several presets. Most of them have more than two colors, and some of them use transparency. Let's try: *Tube Red* and draw some shiny tubes (9).

Now let's make a gradient with some different colors ourselves.

A convenient way to do this is via the *Palettes* panel. I will open the *Palettes* panel by going to the *Configure Tab > Add Tab > Palettes* (10).

In the *Palettes* panel, you can save color *collections*. For example to save the colors of your *brand*, or the colors that you use in a *website*, for quick access.

To create a new color *group* (or *palette*), click at the bottom on the *Create a new Palette* icon (11).

The *Palette Editor* will open. I give my new palette a name, by double-clicking on the text *Untitled*. I type: Gradient test, and press Enter.

In the *Palettes* panel I can already see my new palette displayed: Gradient test(0). The *zero* between parenthesis means that at this moment I have zero colors in my palette.
So let's start adding some colors for our gradient.

I click on the Foreground color to define my first color. I make a yellow.

In the *Palette Editor*, to *add* the yellow to the Palette, I click on the *Create a new entry* icon (12). I have now placed my first color (13).

I click on the Foreground color again to define a new color. I choose green. I click on the *new entry* icon again to add the green. I will also add *blue* and *red*. You can also add the *Background* color to the palette by *Ctrl*-clicking on the *new entry* icon.

To make the preview of the color swatches bigger, first I click on the *Zoom all* magnifying glass at the bottom right (14). Then I drag the panels out to the left (15).

Let's say I *also* want to have red in my gradient at the *beginning*. I can *copy* the red I already have to the first place. To duplicate the red swatch, I drag it to the left (16). I see a *plus* sign, which indicates I am duplicating. The new swatch will be placed at the *left side* of the swatch *above* where I release my mouse (17, 18).

Now I have *five* swatches, because I have duplicated the red swatch.

You can also *edit* a color swatch, by *double*-clicking on it (18). I will change the left red swatch to orange (19).

To *delete* a swatch, select it, and click on the *trash can* (20). I will delete the blue swatch.

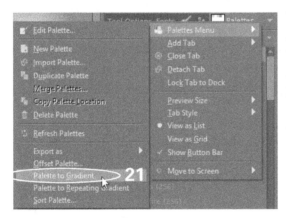

Now I have the colors I want for my gradient.

To turn my palette to a *gradient*, I go to the *Palettes* panel. Here I click on: *Configure this Tab > Palettes Menu > Palette to Gradient* (21).

If I go the *Tool Options*, I can see my new gradient. Let's test it.

I drag over the canvas (22).

Now let's say I want the yellow *area* to be *larger*. To make the yellow area broader, in the *Tool Options* I click on the thumbnail (23). Then, at the bottom right, I click on the *Open the gradient selection dialog* icon (24).

The *Gradients* panel opens. At the bottom left, I click on the *Edit gradient* icon.

Now the *Gradient Editor* opens. To make the *Gradient Editor* panel larger, I drag the panel *out* of the panel group, so it will be a floating panel (25). Then I drag the left side of the panel to the left, to expand the panel (26).

In the *Gradient Editor* we see *black* triangles, and *white* triangles. A black triangle points to a *color*. The white triangles regulate the *transition* between the colors. When a white triangle is in the *middle* of two colors, the transition is *equally* divided, but you can change that.

To make the yellow area broader, I will drag the *other* triangles away (27).

I close the *Gradient Editor* by clicking at the red close button at the top right (28).

To *delete* a gradient, in the *Gradients* panel, select the gradient and click on the *trash* can (28). Then click on *Delete* (29).

In the next lesson we will look at patterns.

43. Making patterns

A pattern is a small image, that is being *repeated* inside an area, until that area is filled up with the pattern.

Open the *Patterns* panel by going to the *Configure Tab > Add Tab > Patterns*. To fill a *layer* with a pattern, simply drag a pattern *icon* on the canvas (1, 2).

I will increase the preview size of the pattern thumbnails, by going to the *Configure Tab > Preview size > Enormous*. Now we can see, patterns can have different sizes. They *don't* have to be *square*, and they can have *transparency*. The patterns at the bottom are Gimps default patterns. The patterns above it, are patterns I have downloaded. At the end of this lesson, I will show you where you can download free patterns.

You can also make a pattern yourself. Let's make a water pattern. Open *Water.jpg*. Crop out a piece of water that looks interesting (3). Next we have to make the pattern *seamless*. This means that the pattern can be repeated, in a way that there will be no transitions visible. I will use a *filter* for this. I go to: *Filters > Map > Make Seamless* (4).

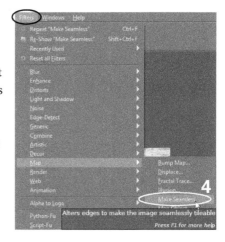

Now the pattern is seamless (5).

To place the pattern in the *Patterns* panel, we have to save it. I go to: *File > Export As*. I will name it `water`. At the bottom, I click on *Select File Type* (5), and scroll down until I see: *GIMP pattern* (6). I select it. At the top I see my file now ends with: *.pat*. I save the pattern

in the *patterns* folder that is inside the .gimp-2.8 folder. At the bottom I click on Export. I type `water` again, and click on Export (7).

Now I click on the *Refresh patterns* button (8) in the *Patterns* panel, and the water pattern is added to the panel. I drag it on the canvas to see the result (9). You can *delete* a pattern, by clicking on the trash can.

I have downloaded several patterns from *textures.com*. You have to subscribe to download textures. I have a free subscription, which gives a limitation in the amount of textures I can download per day.
Let's say I'm looking for a *grass* pattern. At the top there is a search field. I type `grass` (10).

When you hold your mouse above a texture, you can see whether the texture is *seamless*, which means you can directly use it as a pattern (11). When you click on a texture, you can download it. The downloaded file will be a *.jpg* file. Because *.jpg*, *.png*, *.gif*, and *.tiff* files can also be used as a pattern, you can place the jpg file *directly* in the patterns folder of the .gimp-2.8 folder.

In the next lesson we will look at making duotone images.

44. Making duotone images

A duotone image is an image that is built up of two colors, normally a single color, and black. Duotone is often used to create a *sepia effect*, which is a brownish tinted black and white, for an old look.

I have opened *Amsterdam.jpg*. I'll first lighten up the image with Levels.
Now I would like to give this image an old look, a sepia effect. I go to: *Colors > Colorize*. I drag the *Hue* to a brownish color (1). I will *desaturate* the color a bit by dragging *Saturation* to the left (2).

Now let's use duotone to get a modern look. I have opened *Office_buildings.jpg*. I go to: *Colors > Colorize*. I will choose a blue color (3). You can click on *Preview* to compare.

In the last example I will colorize a face by combining *Colorize* and *Curves*. Open *Girl_Close-up.xcf*. I will use green this time. I will first give it maximum *Saturation* (4). I will lower the *Lightness* (5), so I'm not losing too *much* detail in the highlights. I click on OK.
Now I open *Curves*.
I will increase the contrast by giving the curve a *'S'* form (6).
Now I have a cartoony like duotone (7).

In the next lesson we will look at how to save in the PDF format.

45. Saving as a PDF

The PDF format is a globally used format for sharing digital content, that contains both *images* and *text*. PDF stands for *Portable Document Format*. Text in a PDF document can be *real* text (so not pixels). This means text can often be *copied* from a PDF document. The PDF format is not only optimized for viewing on the *screen*, but *also* for *print*. In the printing industry, the PDF format is preferred for printing. Also, regardless which size you print, the *text* will always be sharp.

In Gimp, you can save in the PDF format. Let's create a document with some text, and open it in Acrobat Reader. Create a new document. Select the text tool, and drag a text frame. Type some text.

To save the file as a PDF, go to: *File > Export As*. At the top you can give the file a name. Navigate to the location where you want to save the PDF. At the bottom left click on *Select File Type*. Scroll down to: *Portable Document Format* and click on it. Then click on Export. You're asked if you want to apply layers masks, convert images to vectors, and omit hidden layers. I want the first and last option, and click on Export (1). For complex files with layers that use *blending modes*, it is advisable to first *merge all pixel layers* to a *single layer*, and *above* place the *text layers*, before creating the PDF.

Let's open the PDF in Acrobat Reader. No matter how far we zoom in on the text, the text will *always* stay sharp (2).

In the next lesson we will look at how to save to the Photoshop format.

46. Saving as a Photoshop file

Gimp can *open* Photoshop native .psd files, and *save* Photoshop .psd files. Gimp reads layers, masks, and paths. In the Gimp 3.2 release Gimp will also have layer Styles and Adjustment layers (and probably will be able to read them). For this reason, when you open a .psd file into Gimp that comes from Photoshop, Adjustment layers and layer Styles are ignored, which can be solved by turning layer Styles into *separate layers*, and to *apply* Adjustment layers in Photoshop, before saving a .psd file.

To turn a layer Style, for example a drop shadow, into a separate layer, in Photoshop you *right*-click on the layer Style and choose: *Create Layer* (1). Now the drop shadow is on its own layer (2).

And before you *apply* an Adjustment layer (for example a Levels adjustment) to a layer, *make a copy* of that layer first so you stay flexible and have an original. You can hide the original layer (3).

In Gimp, to *save* in the .psd format, go to: *File > Export As*. At the bottom left click on: *Select File Type*. Scroll down to *Photoshop image*, and select it (4). Now your file name will show .psd at the end. Click on *Export* at the bottom right to save the file. The file can be opened in Photoshop with layers, masks, and paths intact.

In the next chapter we will explore the *Google Nik Collection* plugin suite.

Chapter 5

Google plugins

47. Download and installing

The *Nik Collection* is a *high-end* photo editing plugin suite, used by professional photographers all over the world.

This photo enhancement software comes from a software development company called *Nik Software*, which was established in 1995. The *Nik Collection* suite was originally sold for $500. In 2012 Google acquired Nik Software, to integrate the company into the Google Plus social media platform.

In 2016 Google announced that they will make the entire Nik Collection a *free* download, in order to get unique and powerful photo editing tools, once only used by professionals, out to more people.

The Nik Collection can be downloaded from *www.google.com/nikcollection*. When you click on the download button, you can choose between the *Macintosh* and the *PC* version. After downloading, in your Downloads folder, you can *double*-click on the file to install it (1).

1

nikcollection-full -1.2.11.exe

To open the Nik Collection from *inside* Gimp, we'll install a plugin called *ShellOut.py*. The plugin is written by *Rob Antonishen*. The plugin comes with this lesson. Place the *ShellOut.py* file in the *plug-ins* folder, which is inside the .gimp-2.8 folder.

In the next lesson we will start making global adjustments with Nik's *Viveza 2*.

48. Making global adjustments

The heart of the Nik Collection, is its patented single-click selection method, called *U-Point technology*. Using the U-Point technology, you can select an object, simply by *clicking* on it. The selection you get, gives photo-realistic results. The U-Point technology makes photographic editing fast, easy, and intuitive, as we will see in the *next* lesson.

In this lecture we will explore the interface of the Nik software, and start with making *global* adjustments. In the next lecture, we will look at *local* adjustments using the *U-Point* technology.

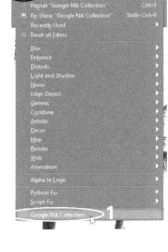

Open *Beach.jpg*. As we can see the image is overexposed. I will open the image in Nik's *Viveza 2*, in which we can adjust Value, color, and structure with easy-to-use sliders.

To open the image in *Viveza 2*, go to: *Filters > Google Nik Collection* (1). In the window that opens, behind *Program*, you can choose a Nik plugin. *DFine 2*, which is a powerful *noise removal* plugin, is shown by default. Click on it, and from the drop-down list, choose *Viveza 2* (2). Behind *Layer* I will leave *new from visible* selected (3). This way I won't overwrite my image, and will receive a *new layer* with the Nik adjustments on it. I click on OK.

When Viveza opens, you can press *F* to work in *full screen mode*. Right now we see four sliders: *Brightness*, *Contrast*, *Saturation*, and *Structure* (4). *Structure* is developed and patented by Nik Software, and we will look at it in a moment.
If you click on the *Expand all sliders* icon (5), you get six more sliders. You can use *all* sliders. To quickly set a slider back to 0%, just *double*-click on the slider triangle.
Warmth works the same way as *temperature* found in programs like *Lightroom*. Dragging it to the left, makes the image look colder, dragging it to the right, makes the image look warmer.

Shadow Adjustments is a powerful way to brighten up the *darkest* areas of an image, like the deep shadows below (7, 8).

With *Structure* you are able to control the amount of *detail* that is visible in an image. Let's see what *Structure* can do for our *overexposed background*. I drag *Structure* to the right (9, 10).

To toggle between a *100%* view, and seeing the *entire* image, just *double*-click on the image. When you press the *spacebar*, you see a *hand* appearing. With the spacebar pressed down, you can pan through the image by *dragging*.

At the top you can click on *Preview*. On the bottom right, click on *Save*. In Gimp, we now get a *new* layer, with the *adjusted* image. Let's compare the sand. We can see the difference that *Structure* has brought (11, 12).

In the next lesson we will start making *local* adjustments using the *U-Point* technology.

49. Making local adjustments

In this lecture we will look at making local adjustments using the *U-Point technology*. Open *Beach_local.jpg*. In this image I want to bring some texture back in the white sand. I go to: *Filters > Google Nik Collection*. I will use *Viveza 2* again.

I want to adjust *only* the sand. To select the sand, I click on the *Add Control Point* button (1). Now I click in the sand. The small circle at the top left, is the *Control point* (2). You can drag the *Control point* around. Below the *Control point* are the same *10 sliders* we also find at the right. And with the *top* slider (at the right of the *Control point*) you can *increase* or *decrease* the *area of influence*, which is the thin circle (3, 4).

Inside this circle, the *sand* is selected. I will increase the *area of influence* by dragging the slider to the right, so that *all* the sand is selected (4). Now I will increase the *Structure* (5). When you click on *Preview* at the top, you can see *only* the sand has been adjusted in the image (selected with just a single click!) (6).

Let's place another *Control point*. I click on the *Add Control Point* button again, and click in the sky (7). I can now lighten the sky, inside the area of influence.

I drag the *Brightness* slider (8). To select more of the sky, I make the *area of influence* larger (9). I can click on the *sand Control point* to work on the sand, and click on the *sky Control point* to work on the sky. If I click on: *Control Point List* at the right (10), I can see my two Control points; *Control Point1*, and *Control Point2*.

I am also able to see the *mask* that *Viveza* has made, by clicking on: *Show / hide selection of Control Point*, at the right of Control point 1 (11).
This is the selection for the *sand* (12).

I deselect the *Show / hide selection of Control Point* for Control point 1, and select it for Control point 2 (13).
We can now see the selection for the *sky* (14).

I will click on *Save*. In Gimp we now have the *original*, and *adjusted* layer. This means we are still able to bring some areas *back* to the original image by using a layer *mask*. I *right*-click on the adjusted layer on top, and choose: *Add Layer Mask*. I fill it with white. If I want to *remove* an adjusted area, I can paint with

black on the mask. If I lower the *Opacity* of the brush, I remove only partially, and start *blending* the layers.

Let's explore *Control points* a bit further. Open *Girl_crop.jpg*. I would like to make the face and the arms of the girl a bit lighter. I go to: *Filters > Google Nik Collection*. This time, I will open the image in *Color Efex Pro 4* (15). Color Efex is a *filter collection* with more that 50 filters. It is used for color corrections, retouching and creative effects.

When you open *Color Efex*, the last filter you used, which in my case is the *Sunlight filter*, is shown at the right (16). We'll look at the *Sunlight filter* in the next lesson.

At the left side you can choose a filter (17). Each filter has several presets, from which you can choose. Click on the *preset mode icon* at the right of a filter (18) to see the presets for that filter.

Click on a preset to use it (19).
To exit the preset mode, click on the *Back* button (20) to go to *list mode* and see all filters displayed again.

Right now we see *all* 55 filters (21). If I click on, for example, the *Landscape* tab, I see the filters that are closely related to Landscape images. I like to see all the filters, so I click on *ALL*.

At the right, I will *remove* the *Sunlight* filter, by clicking on the little *cross* at the right (22). Now I see my image without any adjustments.

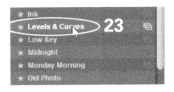

The filter I will use for the image, is *Levels & Curves*. I click on it (23).

In *Color Efex*, the *Control Points* are placed at the bottom of a filter. There are two types of Control Points in Color Efex; *plus* Control Points and *minus* Control Points. The *plus* Control point is a *normal* control point. We will look at the *minus* Control Point in a moment. I click on the *Control Point button* that has a *plus* sign, to add a Control Point (24). I place a Control Point on the girls face, and adjust the area of influence (25).

If I now adjust the Curve at the right (26), I will see I am only adjusting the Value of the grils face. Now let's also brighten up her right arm. I can place a new Control Point, but I can also *reuse* the Control Point I already have, by *duplicating* it.

You can *duplicate* a control point in *three* ways:

1) by pressing *Ctrl-D*
(I can *delete* the duplicate again by pressing *Delete* or *Backspace*).
2) Click on the text: *Control Points*. You now have a *Duplicate* and *Delete* button (27). First select the Control Point you want to duplicate. Then click on the *Duplicate* button (at the left of the trash can).
I will delete the duplicate again.
3) The third way is the *fastest* way. When you hold down *Alt*, and then *drag* a Control Point, you duplicate the Control Point *while you drag!*

I *Alt*-drag the Control Point from the face to the arm, and adjust the area of influence (28). For the arm, I want to *reduce* the *strength* of the effect a bit. In Color Efex a Control Point has an *Opacity* slider (29). I will drag the *Opacity* down to about 70%.

If you experience undesired *spilling* of a *Control Point* to the surroundings, you can do the following. I will drag the Control Point up to the *top* of the arm, and make the area of influence *smaller*, so the Control Point will only cover the top half of the arm. Now I *Alt*-drag this Control Point to the *lower* part of the arm (30). Again I have the whole arm covered, but now I am using *two smaller* Control Points to do this, which leads to less spilling.

To adjust the light on this *arm*, it would be efficient to have *both* Control Points to *act as one*. I can do this by *grouping* the Control Points. To *group* Control Points, I start by selecting the Control Points that I want to group. You select Control Points by *Shift*-clicking on them. The *first selected* Control Point becomes the Control Point that will control the *other* Control Points of the group. When you have all Control Points selected, click on the *Click to group the selected Control Points* button (31).

I now have a *group* of Control Points, named: *Group1* (32).

If I now adjust the *main* (the first selected) Control Point (33), I am also changing the *other* Control Point (34).

If you want to *ungroup* a group again, select the group (35), and click on the *Click to ungroup Control Points* button (36).

I will also *Alt*-drag a Control Point over to the girl's *left* arm.

Now let's have a look at the *minus Control Point*. We've seen how to *combine smaller* Control Points to minimize the spill, if needed. If this wouldn't be enough, you can also use *minus* Control Points. To show how they work, we will look at the *masks* themselves. At the right I click on *Show / hide selection for all Control Points* (37). We now can see the masks (38).

You can *show* and *hide* *individual* Control Points, by clicking on the *Show / hide selection of Control Point* icons. Let's hide the Control Point for the *face* (39, 40). I will reveal the selection of the face again, by clicking on the icon again.

To remove the light spill we have, I will now place a *minus* Control Point. I click on the *Add a Control Point set to 0% Opacity* button (41), and then I click at the *left* of the girls face. I will increase the area of influence (42).

I can do the same at the bottom. I click on the *minus* Control Point button again, and click at the right of her arm (43). And lastly, I place a minus Control Point at the left side of her arm, to subtract from the selection (44). I click twice on the *Show / hide selection for all Control Points* icon, to exit mask view again.

Now I have a very refined mask. If I adjust the curve (45), I see *only* the face and arms are affected (46).

Now let's say I want to make the skin tone a bit *warmer*. I could go into the *Red*, *Green* and *Blue* color channels of the filter and adjust them (47), but I will use *another filter* for this; the *Brilliance / Warmth* filter. You can *add* a new filter in *two* ways. The first method is to click (below the filters at the right) on the *Add Filter* button (48). Then go to the left side and choose a filter by clicking on it. I'll *delete* the placed filter again by clicking on the little cross (49). With the second method you can *skip* the *Add Filter* button, and directly add a new filter by *Shift*-clicking on it. When you use this second method to add a filter, be careful not to click on a filter *without* holding Shift, because this will *remove* the last added filter. When this happens you can press *Ctrl-Z* to undo.

I will use the fast method, and *Shift*-click on *Brilliance / Warmth* (50). The filter is now added to the filter list. There is also a *History panel* (51). Click on the tab to open it. I will drag the slider to the bottom. We can see the *last* action is: *Brilliance /*

Warmth added (52). Like in Gimp, you can *select* an *earlier* state, and continue from there. To exit the *History Panel*, click at the top on the Color Efex Pro 4 tab.

What I would like to do is to *reuse* the Control Points that I made with Levels and Curves. To do this, I go to Levels and Curves.

To select *all* Control Points, I can *drag* over the entire image, or I can press *Ctrl-A* (which is faster). To *copy* the selected Control Points, I click on the menu icon at the right (53), and choose: *Copy Control Points*.

Now I go to *Brilliance / Warmth*. I click on the menu icon at the right of Brilliance / Warmth, and choose: *Paste Control Points* (54). I have now *copied* the Control Points over.

When I drag the Warmth slider to the right (55), I am *only* making the *skin* warmer. I can *show* and *hide* the Brilliance / Warmth filter by clicking on the *check mark* at the left of the filter name (56).

To *zoom in* press the space bar. To *zoom out*, press the space bar again. You can change the *zoom percentage* at the top by clicking on the triangle icon (57). To *pan*, like in *Viveza 2*, hold the spacebar pressed down, and drag with your mouse.

50. Using recipes

If I want to continue working on the image at a later point, I can save my work as a *Recipe*. The *Save Recipe* button is at the bottom right (1). I can save in two ways: *with*, or *without* the Control Points included. To save *with* the Control Points, press *Shift* when you click on the *Save Recipe* button. I will *Shift*-click on the button.

I type a name for the *Recipe* (2), and click on OK.

The *Recipes menu* opens at the left. My *Recipe* (called `Girl`) is displayed (3).

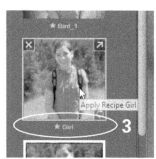

Now I can continue working on the image at a later point. My settings are saved. At the bottom right I click on *Save* (4), to open the image in Gimp.

An image saved from *Color Efex* will give a *TIFF image Message* (5). The message tells that the image has been transferred from *Color Efex* to *Gimp* in the high quality *TIFF* format (which is what we want). You can just press the *space bar* and the message disappears.

Now let's say I want to *continue* working in *Color Efex* with my image. Because the *top visible* layer will be opened when you use a Google filter, you can either drag the *original* layer to the top (6), or hide the layer(s) above it.

I go to *Filters > Google Nik Collection*. The last filter that I used *(Color Efex)* is still selected, so I click on OK. I go to the *Recipes*, I click on the saved *Recipe* called `Girl`. I'm warned that the *Recipe* will *replace* any *current* filters at the right (7). I click on Yes. Now I can continue working on the image, with my *saved settings*.

Click to update this recipe

When I'm finished and leave Color Efex, and I want to *save* my settings *again*, I can:

1) create a *new* Recipe, or
2) I can *update* the *existing* Recipe.

To *update* a Recipe, click on the *update button* at the bottom right of the Recipe Thumbnail (8).

I can also *delete* a Recipe, by clicking at the *top left* (9). And I can *save* a Recipe on my hard drive, for *back-up* and for *sharing*, by clicking on the *top right* (10).

In the next lesson we will explore some more *filters* in *Color Efex Pro 4*.

51. Adjusting color and structure

Color Efex Pro has 55 filters. Google has a Nik Collection *YouTube* channel, where each filter of Color Efex is discussed separately. You can find the YouTube channel at: *www.youtube.com/user/NikSoftwareLessons*
You can also visit Googles website: *the Nik Collection by Google Help Center* at: *https://support.google.com/nikcollection.*

In this lesson I will discuss some filters to get you started. I start with three filters that make images look warmer.

In the last lecture we've already used the *Brilliance / Warmth* filter to warm up the skin of the girl.
A filter related to it, is the *Sunlight Filter*.
Open *Sun_forest.jpg*. I would like to add some sunlight to this image. I select the *Sunlight* filter (1).
I can adjust the *Light Strength*, the *Light Temperature*, as well as the *Brightness*, *Contrast*, and *Saturation*.
We now have a sunnier image (2).

The next warming filter is the *Skylight Filter* (3).
Open *Woman_beach.jpg*. The *Skylight Filter* removes blue casts and warms the image up (4).

With the *Foliage Filter* (5), you can bring the *greens* in nature images, to life. There are three presets. I will choose *Method 2*. With *Enhance Foliage* you can set the strength of the filter.

Now we will look at two interesting *color correction* filters. Open *Bride.jpg*. To color correct this image, and remove the *blue color cast* from the wedding dress, I will select the *White neutralizer filter*. At the right, I select the color picker (6). When I click on the dress (7), the blue color cast will be removed (8). At the left of the color picker, I can see the color I have chosen to become *neutral*. The *White neutralizer filter* is more flexible than the *Pick grey point* picker from *Levels* in Gimp.

Another interesting color correction filter is *Remove Color Cast* (9). Open *Town.jpg*. By dragging the Color slider, you can quickly find the best point for *neutralising* the color cast.

In the previous lesson we've seen *Structure* in action in *Viveza*. *Color Efex* goes further, and offers *six contrast* filters, which are all based on the *Structure* algorithm. Let's have a look.

If you want a more dramatic look in an image, you can use *Dark contrasts* (10). Open *mountains_snow.jpg*. I will increase *Contrast*, *Dark Detail*, and *Brightness*. With *Shadows / Highlights protection*, you can reduce the effect in the Shadows and/or Highlights if needed.

The next filter is *Contrast Only*. Open *Rose.jpg*. With *Contrast Only* you have control over *how* contrast is applied. You have *Normal Contrast* (11) followed by *Contrast Only* (12), which prevents

colors from being *affected*, and *Soft Contrast* (13), which gives *softer transitions*. When I select the *Dark Contrasts* (14) filter, we see we get a totally different result. *Contrast Only* is often used for food photography.

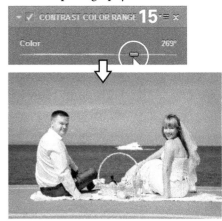

Another contrast filter is *Contrast color range* (15). I have opened *Bride_and_groom.jpg*.

The color selected with *Color*, will cause objects of that color to become *lighter*, while opposite, or *complementary* colors will become *darker*. This is a quick and effective way, to get better contrast between the bride and groom, and the background.

With *Dark contrasts*, we made *lighter* areas *darker*, to give them more drama. With *Pro Contrast*, we do the opposite, and dynamically *lighten up* areas in a *dark image*.

I have opened *Flowers.jpg*. We can see the flowers much better now (16).

With *Detail extractor*, you can bring out detail in an image in *three* ways. Open *Ocean_rocks.jpg*. Under *Effect Radius*, you can adjust the *fine* detail (17), the *medium* detail (18), or the *Larger* detail (19) *separately*.

And finally, with *Tonal contrast*, you can bring out detail in the *Highlights*, *Midtones*, or *Shadows* separately. There are also *five* Contrast Types you can choose from: *Standard* (20), *High Pass* (21), *Fine* (22), *Balanced* (23), and *Strong* (24).

In this lesson, we have used the filters globally. For more *refined* results, you can use the *Control Points*.

In the next lesson we will look at *creative* filters.

52. Using creative filters

To get a different look and feel for your
image, *Color Efex* has several creative
filters, like the *Bleach bypass* filter.
Open *Pub.jpg*. The Bleach bypass filter
simulates a technique from the days of
color film, where the bleaching step
was skipped. This results in a high
contrast, low saturation look (1).

For more creative filters, we will now go to *Analog Efex Pro 2*,
which is the plugin for special effects. This plugin can be very
useful for giving a *book cover* a special look. Open *The man on the
train.xcf*. I *right*-click on the top layer and choose: *New from Visible*,
(2) to get a single layer I can open in *Analog Efex*. Then I go to: *Filters >
Google Nik Collection*. I choose *Analog Efex Pro 2*, and click on OK.

At the left, there are some presets (3). From the presets we can already get
some interesting ideas for an effect, which can then be fully modified at the
right side. *Analog Efex*, like *Color Efex*, works with *stackable* effects.

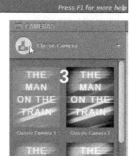

To get to the *individual* filters, click on the *Classic Camera* icon (4).

Below *Tools*, we see the
filters of *Analog Efex*.
Let's have a look at
Light Leaks (5).
I click on it.

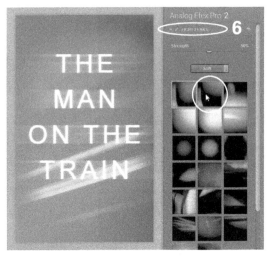

With *Light Leaks* (6) you can add a *light flare* to your image.

There are many Light Leaks to choose from. There are: *Soft*, *Crisp*, and *Dynamic* leaks (7).

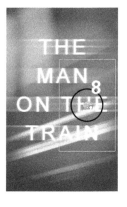

You can *position* a light leak, by dragging the blue circle (8).

At the top, you can set the *Strength* of the Light Leak (9).

As in Color Efex, you will *replace* an effect if you click on another affect at the left. To *add* an effect in Analog Efex, you click on the *plus* icon, at the right of an effect (10). I will add: *Zoom & Rotate Blur*.

To remove an effect, click on the *minus* icon (11).

With *Zoom & Rotate Blur*, I can bring some movement to text and images. The inner circle is the *effect free area* (12), and between the inner and outer circle is the *transition* area (13).

I can adjust the *size* of the *inner*, and the *outer* circle (14, 15). I can also *rotate* the *outer* circle (16).

I can reposition the whole effect with the blue middle point (17).

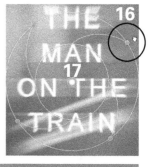

I can also use the *sliders* at the right (18).

Because I want to distort *only* the *text*, and *not* the background, I'll press Cancel. In Gimp, I delete the top layer (that Analog Efex returned). I want to make a layer with *only* text visible, on a *black* background. To do this, I place *above* the layer(s) that I don't want to be distorted an new layer, and fill it with black. Above this black layer I place the *text* layers that I want to adjust. Then I *right*-click on the top layer, and choose: *New from Visible*. Now I have a *single* layer with *only* text, on a *black* background (19). The black background will *disappear* later again, when I set the result (coming from Analog Efex) on the *Screen* blending mode. Doing this, I am able to place the

adjusted text in front of the unaffected image(s).

I go to: *Filters > Google Nik Collection*, and click on OK. I click on the *Classic Camera* icon, and select the *Zoom & Rotate Blur* filter. I will add some motion to the text. Then I click on Save.

In Gimp I will now *hide* the *original* text layers (for backup). I will also delete the *black* layer, and the *New from Visible* layer. I set the layer that *Analog Efex* returned, on the *Screen* blending mode. Now we see the result (20).

Next, let's add some motion to an *image*. For a thriller book-cover, I open *Barn.jpg*. I go to: *Filters > Google Nik Collection*, and open *Analog Efex*. I click on the *Classic Camera* icon, and select the *Zoom & Rotate Blur* filter again.

I drag the midpoint on the tree (21) and rotate the blur a bit. I click on Save.

A related blur effect is *Motion blur*. Open *Race_car.jpg*. I would like to bring some motion blur into this image. I go to: *Filters > Google Nik Collection*, and open *Analog Efex*. I click on the *Classic Camera* icon, and select the *Motion Blur* filter. As with *Zoom & Rotate Blur*, you have the *effect free* area (22), and the *transition* area (23). With the small circle (24) you set *both* the direction (or *Angle*), *and* the *Strength* of the motion blur (longer distance means stronger blur). Independent of this *main* blur control, you can also add *seven additional* Blur Points, to tweak the result. With these additional Blur Points, you can control the Angle and Strength in a certain *area* (25). To delete an additional Blur Point, select it and press *Delete*.

I have already *saved* a finished motion blur effect for this race car (26). The *preset*, which is called a *Recipe* in Color Efex, can be found in the *Custom* panel. I named my Recipe: Race-car. I click on it (26).
I have placed the main control at the top (27), and used all seven additional Blur Points, to tweak the result locally.
To have the *driver free* of blur, I placed a blur point *on* the driver, and dragged the dot at the end of the arrow *fully in*.

To *save* a *preset* in *Analog Efex*, click on the *Save* preset button (28). Like in *Color Efex*, to save a preset with Control Points included, you *Shift*-click. And you can also *update*, *delete*, and *export* the preset.

Finally, we will look at *Bokeh*. Open *Town_at_night.jpg*. Go to: *Filters > Google Nik Collection*, and open *Analog Efex*.

Again, there is an *effect free* area, and a *transition* area (29).

You can change the look of the bokeh (30).

I click on Save. In Gimp I will remove the bokeh at the top of the tower with a layer *mask*. I *right*-click, choose: *Add Layer Mask*, and choose white. I paint with a large soft brush with black in the layer mask (31).

I have now added some depth to my image using the *Bokeh* filter (32).

In the next lesson we will look at making Vignettes.

53. Making vignettes

A vignette normally is a darkening of the edges of an image. It can be added to draw the attention of the viewers eye to the subject in the middle. In this lesson we will look at some vignette filters and image borders in *Color Efex*. Open *Bird_1.jpg*. Go to: *Filters > Google Nik Collection*, and open *Color Efex*.

At the left, select *Vignette Filter*. *Transition* (1) is the distance between the *inner* and *outer* circle, as we saw in *Analog Efex*.

If I drag the *Transition* slider to the left, I get a smaller transition area (2). With *Size* I adjust the size of the effect *free* area (the *inner* circle). With *Opacity* I adjust the strength, or *opacity* of the vignette. With *Shape* (3), you can choose different shapes for the vignette.

You can adjust the *color* of the vignette.
With the *color picker* (4) you can pick a color from your image (5). If you click on the color *thumbnail* (6), you can manually *adjust* the color. From left to right is *Hue* (7), from top to bottom is *Saturation* (8). And at the right is the *Value* slider, with which you can make a color lighter or darker (9).

Adapt Edges looks at the image and tries to *refine the shape* for the vignette.

For the second vignette filter, *Vignette Lens*, open *Bird_2.jpg*. *Vignette Lens* simulates natural vignettes created by different types of *lenses*. I can transition the Shape from more Circular (10) to

more Rectangular (11). I can adjust the *Size* of the vignette. With *Amount* I can make the vignette darker, or *lighter*. As a result, I can *invert* the vignette, creating a *light vignette* (12).

I can *reposition* the *center* of the vignette. I click on the *Place Center* icon (13), and click in the middle of the bird (14).

I can also place a *minus control point* to *remove* an area of the vignette. I click on the *minus control point* icon, and click on the *eye* of the bird (15).

Another vignette filter is *Vignette blur*. Open *Portrait.jpg*. With *Vignette blur*, you *defocus* the detail around the center of the image, drawing the eye to the subject.

There are four different blur types you can choose from. *Type 4* blurs to white (16, 17).

17

I will make the transition a bit *less soft* (18), and increase the size a bit.

I click on the *Place Center icon*, and click on her face, to put the girl in the center of the vignette (19). In Gimp, I could *crop* the image again.

19

20

The *Darken / Lighten center* vignette filter is a much more *subtle* way of vignetting. It gives *depth* to an image in a *natural* way.
With *Border Luminosity* you can darken or lighten the edges of the image (20). And with *Center Luminosity* you determine the brightness of the center of the image.
With *Center Size* you make the border smaller or larger.

21

Apply Recipe Vintage Saturation

★ Vintage Saturation

Color Efex also has some adjustable *image borders*. I click on the *Recipes* tab. At the bottom I select *Vintage Saturation* (21). I get a warning that adding this Recipe will replace the filters at the right (22). I click on Yes.

Warning

22

Adding a Recipe will replace all filters currently applied to your image. Would you like to continue?

Do not show again   NO   YES

This Recipe has four filters working together. On top the image is given more *contrast*. Below is *Vignette Lens*, to give the image a vignette. Then we have an *image border*. And at the bottom we can see that also *Film Grain* has been added.

Let's take a look at *Film Grain*.

I will zoom in to 200%. I can increase the size of the *grain* if I want to, by dragging *Grain per pixel* to the left (23).

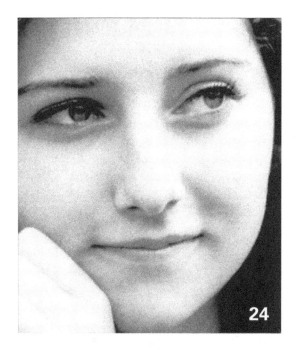

The grain makes the image look like it was shot with *film* (24).

Above *Film Grain* are the *Image borders*. There are 14 image borders to choose from.

You can make an image border more rough or less rough (25). With *Spread* you can *thicken* the edge (26).
And with *Size*, you can move the edge inwards or outwards (27).

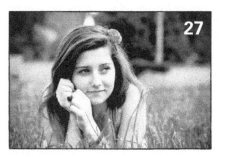

In the next lesson we will look at how to make black and white images in *Silver Efex Pro*.

54. Making black and white images

Silver Efex Pro is often considered to be the most powerful black and white plugin on the market, and is used by many professional photographers. With *Silver Efex Pro*, you can make professional looking black and white images, in just a few clicks. Open *Castle.jpg*. Open *Silver Efex Pro*. By default you get a *neutral* black and white conversion (1). By dragging the *Structure* slider, the detail of the image comes out (2).

If I click on the triangle in front of *Contrast* (3), I get *more options* for adjusting Contrast. I can now amplify the *whites* and *blacks* separately.

I will amplify the *blacks* a bit (4, 5). I will also add some *Soft Contrast* (6), to bring more *depth* to the image (7).

To compare, I can not only click on the *Compare* button, but I can also select *Split preview* (8). I can now drag a *red line* to the left and the right (9), which lets me quickly compare the before and after. At the right of Split preview is *Side-by-side* preview (10).
In between the images, you can click on the *double arrow* to alternate between seeing the images on top of each other (11),

or side by side (12). Split preview and Side-by-side preview are also available in the other Nik plugins.
To create more room for the image, you can *hide* (and show) the tab columns at both sides individually, by clicking on the *Show / Hide icons* (at the left and right side).

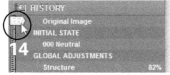

I can also compare to the (original) *color* image. To do this, I click on the *History* tab, and drag the orange slider (13) to the top, to: *Original Image* (14).
To be able to drag the *orange slider* in the History panel, you need to be in *Split preview* or *Side-by-side preview*.

Now let's do something more challenging. Open *Bride_and_groom.jpg*. Go to: *Filters > Google Nik Collection*, and open *Silver Efex*. As we can see, there is not much contrast between the bride and groom, and the background.

I click on *Color Filter*. Here I can add different color filters. Let's see how they affect the image. Grey is neutral, as we have now. If I use the *Red* (15) or *Yellow* filter, the bride and groom brighten up (16).

Now I click on *Film Types* (17) and open *Sensitivity* (18). Here I can control *per color*, how dark or light that color will be. Dragging to the left makes it darker, to the right brighter. I will increase the *Red* tones, which brightens up the *skin* tones (19). I will also increase *Cyan* and *Blue* to brighten up the *sky* and the *water*. And lastly, I will increase the *Structure* a bit. I click on Save.

In Gimp, I could *also use* this black and white image, to improve the *color* image! I will set it's blending mode to *Value* (20). By adjusting the Opacity, I can determine how *much* I want to *replace* the *Value* from the color layer, with the *improved* Value from the black and white layer (21).

I can even lighten up the *Value* layer a bit with *Levels*. By hiding the top layer, I can see the improvement of the light conditions for the bride and groom.

I will create a single image from the result, by *right*-clicking on the top layer, and choose *New from visible*. I open *Color Efex*. I will use the *Sunlight filter* to give the image a bit more sun, and click on Save. In Gimp can *lower* the Opacity a bit if I want. If I *Shift*-click on the eye of the bottom layer (the layer that I started with) I can now see how the image has improved from the start.

In the next lesson we will look at reducing digital noise with DFine.

55. Remove noise

In this lesson we will look at reducing digital noise. Open *Girl_crop.jpg*.
Go to: *Filters > Google Nik Collection*, and open *DFine 2*. When you open
the program it will already have already *analysed* and *denoised* the image.
It analysed the noise by looking at a couple of low contrast areas. The
program shows where it looked, which is *inside* the *white* dotted *squares*
(1). Nine out of ten times, this *automatic* noise reduction will give good
results, and you can directly click on Save.

However, if you want to, you have more
control. You can for example draw your *own*
squares (or rectangles) for the program to
look at. To do this, behind *Method*, click on
Automatic, and choose: *Manual* (2). Below,
you can now click on the *Add rectangle* button
(3), and drag over an important area,
that you want to be *denoised* (4).

Add rectangle

If you click on the *Select* tool (5), you can *move*
and *resize* the rectangles. You can also *delete*
rectangles by selecting them and pressing the
Delete key. To delete *all* rectangles click on the
Reset button.

When you *change* a rectangle, the program
will say: *Profile needs to be updated* (6).
To make a *new* profile from the *new*
rectangles, click on the *Measure Noise*
button (7).

To *zoom* in and out I select the *Zoom* tool (8). My
cursor changes to a *magnifying glass* with a *plus* sign
(9). If I now click, I zoom in to 300%. To zoom *out*
again, I press the *Alt* key, which turns the
magnifying glass into a *minus* sign (10). If I now
click with the minus sign, I am back to 100%.

If I click one *more* time with the *Alt* key pressed down, I will see the *whole*
image. I release the *Alt* key again, and click twice on the girls face to zoom in
to 300%.

I click on *Preview*, to see the before and after (11, 12). I think the denoising is a little bit too strong on the face, but could be stronger for the background (because the background is *out of focus*, and doesn't have detail).

When I read: *Automatic profile applied*, or, *Manual profile applied* (13), I can adjust the denoising by clicking on the *Reduce* button (14).
I can now choose between two methods to adjust the result. I can use *Control points*, or: *Color Ranges*. Let's start with *Color Ranges* (15).

I will click on the top color picker (16), and then click on the cheek of the girl. I have now selected a skin tone (17).

With the *Contrast Noise* slider (18) I now can *decrease* or *increase* the applied noise reduction for *just* the *chosen* color. I will drag the *Contrast Noise* slider to the left (so *under* 100%), to *reduce* the applied noise reduction for the *skin tones*. When I would go *above* 100%, I would *increase* the applied noise reduction for the selected color, even *more*.

Contrast Noise effectively reduces *differences* in *Value* of the selected color. *Color Noise* reduction (the slider below) is less noticeable, especially in *jpeg* images, due to the *jpeg compression*.

Now I select the *second* color picker, and click in the green. I will *increase* the noise reduction for the green tones, because they are in the *background*, which is out of focus. You can *add* more color ranges when needed, by clicking on the *plus* icon at the bottom (19).

You can also use *Control points* to adjust the applied noise reduction. The advantage of *Control points* is that you can easily *exclude* areas from being denoised. By using *minus* Control points I can for example exclude the eyes and eyebrows (where the denoising is a bit to strong). I click on the *minus* Control point button (20).

Then I click on the eye, and decrease the area of influence (21).

I *Alt*-drag the *Control point* to the other eye. And I also duplicate it for the eyebrows. The eyes and eyebrows are now *excluded* from the denoising.

At the right *side* of the nose (in the shadow), I want to *increase* the denoising. To do this I place a normal *(plus)* Control point in the shadow area, and *increase Contrast Noise* by dragging the *Contrast Noise slider* of the Control point to the right (22).

You *deselect* Control points by clicking beside them on the canvas.

After placing the Control points, I am *still* able to increase or decrease the *overall* noise reduction. Let's say I now want to *denoise* the entire image *stronger* (so more than 100%). I do this by dragging the *main Contrast Noise* slider to the right (23). This will not affect the eyes and eyebrows.

In the next lesson we'll look at how to sharpen an image with Sharpener Pro.

56. Sharpening images

In this lecture we will look at how to sharpen an image with *Sharpener Pro 3*. Open *Girl_hair.xcf*. Go to: *Filters > Google Nik Collection*. Under *Program*, we do not only find the *Sharpener* plugin, but also a *pre*-sharpener. The *pre*-sharpener is also called *RAW image sharpener*, and is *only* meant for *RAW* images. RAW is a photo format used by professional photographers. Because RAW images aren't *pre*-sharpened by the camera (like a jpeg is), RAW images first need to be *pre*-sharpened. For more information about pre-sharpening RAW images visit: *www.youtube.com/user/NikSoftwareLessons*.

I open *Sharpener Pro 3*. With *Adaptive Sharpening* (1) you set the *strength* of the sharpening (from 0% to 100%). Below, you determine *how* you sharpen. You can adjust: *Structure*, *Local Contrast*, and *Focus*. I will leave *Adaptive Sharpening* at 100%. Below, with *Output Sharpening Strength*, I can reduce or increase the sharpening strength by dragging the slider below or above 100%. *Higher* than 100% means *increasing* the strength even more.

Right now the image is sharpened. However, I see some noise I don't want. I will *decrease* Structure a bit to reduce the appearance of too much *fine detail*, resulting in smoother surfaces. I will *increase* Local Contrast a bit. Focus *does* make the image sharper, but also introduces the noise again, so I will leave it at 0%.

I click on Preview to see the result. The image has become sharper (2).

I can see a light *halo* around the stars in the shadow of the shirt (3). I will place a *Control point*, to *reduce* the halos. I click on the *Add Control Point* button (4), and click on the shadow (*not* on a star!). I adjust the area of influence (5). Now I drag the *Output Sharpening Strength* of the Control point to 0%.

I have now *excluded* the shadow of the shirt from being sharpened. As a result, the halos have disappeared. Because I *only* selected the *shadow* of the shirt, the stars are still sharpened!

When we take a look at the *mask* of the Control point (6), we can see the starts are *not* selected by the Control point. This means they are *not* affected by dragging the *Output Sharpening Strength* of the Control point to 0%.

The girl improved by the sharpening, but I liked the background better of the *original*. Back in Gimp, I can quickly restore the background using a layer *mask* (7).

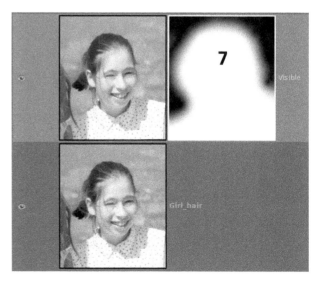

In the next lesson we will look at HDR photography.

57. What is HDR photography?

We've come to the last plugin of the Nik Collection, which is *HDR Efex Pro*. Open *Room_inside.xcf*.

The image of the room has been constructed in *HDR Efex*; it is namely build up from *two* other images. We can see that in this image, *both* the inside of the room, *and* the outside, are well lit.

However, when we look at the original images that I made with my camera, we can see the camera *originally* wasn't able to shoot this.

1

When I set the camera to have the *inside* well lit, the outside is blown out (1).
And when I focus the camera on having the *outside* well lit, the inside becomes *very* dark (2). Why is this?

2

The reason for this, is that our *eyes* are about twice as flexible as a camera is. This means, our eyes are able to see a much *wider* range of very dark, up until very light colors (3), than a camera can (4).

Normally this isn't a problem, and isn't noticeable. But in some situations, for example with a very bright *sun* in the background, combined with deep *shadow* areas, the lower *dynamic range* of the camera can become visible. The deepest blacks, up until the lightest lights, now *can't* be captured by a normal camera *all* at the *same time*. So when you want in a HDR (*High Dynamic Range*) situation, to capture an image that exactly shows what you see with your eyes, you have to make more than one picture. A darker picture, and a lighter picture. Then you *combine* these images in a HDR program.
When you make more than one picture of the same scene, you will need a tripod, to make sure the camera doesn't move between making the different pictures.

If you don't have a tripod, or you have only *one* image from a scene, you can *still* open a single image in *HDR Efex* to improve it. You will get better results though, using different images that together cover the whole light spectrum. When you open a single image, it's best to open a *darker* image, so *without blown out* highlights. Dark areas (because they are still visible) can be recovered to a certain extent. Let's open the *dark* image of the room. I go to: *Filters > Google Nik Collection*, and choose *HDR Efex Pro*. With the default settings, the image improved a lot (5). However the colors suffer to some extent from the image being underexposed, and don't look that natural.

Now let's open *multiple* images of the room. The opening of

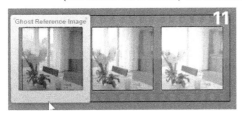

multiple images goes via the plugin itself. I go to: *File > Open images* (6).

Although you can create an HDR image with just *two* images, HDR programs *prefer* a minimum of *three* images, so with an *extra neutral* image in between the dark, and light image. I have also added a neutral image. I hold the *Ctrl* key pressed down, and select *Room_dark.jpg*, *Room_medium.jpg*, and *Room_light.jpg* (7). I click on Open.

In the *Merge dialog* window, I will check all three options at the right. The images will now be *Aligned* (8), and color artefacts (*Chromatic Aberration*) are removed (9). When *Ghost Reduction*

is checked (10), at the top you can choose *which* image will be the *Ghost Reference Image* (11).
You can choose the *Ghost Reference Image* by dragging the lighter frame over it (12). The *Ghost Reference Image* determines *where* an object will be visible (e.g. a driving car, or a walking person), when that object has *moved* between shooting the images.

At the bottom (13), you can adjust the *relative* influence of the images by dragging the scroll bar. I will leave it as it is, so *equally* divided. I click on *Create HDR*.

Under *Tonality* (14), I can adjust the *Exposure* to make the image lighter or darker. I will make the image a bit lighter by dragging to the right. I can also adjust the *Shadows* and *Highlights* individually.

Below, I can adjust the *Contrast* (15), and the *Structure* (16).

With *Tone Compression* (17) I can bring the *Value* (dark and light) tones *closer* to each other. Moving the slider to the right makes *light* tones *darker*, and *dark* tones *lighter*, trying to make all Value tones more *equal*.

Method Strength (18) determines how *strong* the settings, that are below HDR Method, are applied. Right now *Depth* (19) is set to *Normal*. I can increase it to *Strong*, or decrease it to *Subtle*.
Detail is by default on *Realistic* (20). To the left makes the detail *softer*, and to the right makes it *stronger*.
Drama (21) is a creative effect. You can give the image a more dramatic look.

Under *Color* (22) you can adjust *Saturation*, color *Temperature*, and *Tint*. *Tint* in conjunction with *Temperature* is often used in programs as Lightroom to *color correct* an image.

Under *Selective Adjustments* you can place *Control Points* to add masks.
Under *Finishing*, you have the *Graduated Neutral Density Filter* (23).
When you have a landscape image where the bright sky is *still* too light,
you can selectively *darken* the top of the image without darkening the rest
of the image. If you drag *Upper tonality* (24) to the left, you darken the top
of the image (25). You can also darken (or lighten) the lower part of the image
with *Lower Tonality*. With *Blend*, you can make the *transition area* larger or
smaller.
With *Vertical Shift*, you can move the whole transition *up*, or *down*.
And with *Rotation*, you can *rotate* the whole filter.
In *Color Efex*, there are several *Graduated Neutral Density Filters* you can use.

To save an image from HDR Efex, whether it is coming from *multiple* images,

or from a *single* image opened via
Gimp, you have to save *via the plugin
itself.*
I go to: *File > Save Image As* (26).
I give the file a name (27). I can save
the file as a JPG, or as a TIF. JPG uses
lossy compression, so I will choose TIF
(28). In Gimp, I will open the TIF file,
saved from *HDR Efex*.

In the next chapter we will look at Retouching.

Chapter 6

Retouching

58. Using the Clone tool

In this chapter we will look at retouching techniques, and the different tools that are available for this.

We start with the *Clone* tool (1). With the *Clone* tool you can copy an area of your image and paste it onto another area. This technique is often used to *remove elements* from an image.

Open *Organ.jpg*. In this image I want to remove a wire at the left of the organ. I click on the *Clone* tool, or press *S* (from *Stamp*). I zoom in to about 300% to have a good view. In the *Tool Options* I will choose a soft brush with 0% hardness. I set the size of the brush to 20 by *Alt*-scrolling. With the *Clone* tool, I will now *copy* pixels from the environment on top of the wire, to make the wire 'disappear'.

To work *non-destructively*, I will work on an *empty* layer *above* the image (2). This way, the cloned pixels (coming from the layer below) are placed on *another* layer, so no pixels are overwritten. The reason I am *able* to clone pixels *from other* layers (than the layer that I am actually working on; the empty layer on top), is because in the Tool Options, *Sample merged* has been activated (3). With *Sample merged* checked, everything that is *visible*, is treated as a *single* layer.

What I want, is to *copy* the pixels that are inside the Clone brush (4), and place them *over* the wire.
To do this I first *Ctrl*-click on the place, where I want to copy the pixels from (5). If I now move my mouse to the left (6), I get a *second* circle. The second circle shows me, *where* the pixels from the *first* circle are going to be placed, if I start drawing.

In the first circle (5) you will get to see a little *cross* in the middle of the circle when you hold down the *Ctrl* key. In the second circle (6) you will always see a white *arrow* (that points to the middle of the circle). The cross and the arrow help with *aligning*. Let's say I will use the *horizontal* edge of the beam for *aligning*.
I hold down the *Ctrl* key, and position the *horizontal* line of the cross on the edge of the beam (5). Then I click. Now I release the *Ctrl* key. I move my mouse to the left (6). Inside my second circle, I will point the white arrow to the *same* edge, so that the content of the circles will be perfectly *aligned*.

Now I click and drag over the wire (7). I release my mouse. I will also paint over the wire below (8). I have now made a piece of the wire disappear.

Because I have cloned on a *separate* layer, my *original* layer is still intact.

Now let's have a look at the difference between cloning with a *soft* brush, and a *hard* brush.

At the top left, I will remove a pin that's in the wall (9). I zoom in to 300%, and set the brush size to 30. I will first remove the pin with a *soft* brush.

To *align* the clone, I will take the sample at the *top left corner* of a brick (10), and start cloning from the *top left corner* of another brick (11).

Now I draw over the pin (12). The result with a soft brush looks good.

Now let's do the same with a *hard* brush. By pressing *Ctrl-Z* I undo the cloning.

To get a hard brush, I don't have to change my brush. I can temporarily select *Hard edge* in the *Tool Options* (13).

I draw over the pin again. We can see the difference: the hard edge is *visible* (14). Normally, the *larger* the brush, the *softer* the brush needs to be. When you work with a *very small* brush, like size 10, a *hard* brush is the better choice.

In the next lesson, we will let Gimp remove a piece of wire.

59. Remove objects with Heal Selection

We can also let Gimp remove an object for us, using the *Heal selection* filter. Open *Organ.jpg*. Let's remove the wire at the top.

I press *Ctrl-1* to get a 100% view. I tell Gimp which area I want to be removed, by placing a *selection* around it. I click on the *Free Select* tool, and click around the wire to select it (1). I go to: *Filters > Enhance > Heal Selection*.

Context sampling width (pixels) (2) determines how far, *around* the selection, the program will look to copy material from. I will leave it at 50 pixels. *Sample from* (3) is by default on *All around*. You can also choose to sample from just the *Sides* (so from just the left and right side of the selection), or from *Above and below*. This choice depends on the situation. I will sample from *All around*.

Filling order (4) is normally best left on *Random*. We will explore *Filling order* further in the next example. I click on OK.

I press *Ctrl-D* to deselect.

The wire has been removed (5).

Now open *Lotus.xcf*. In this image (6), I would like to place more focus on the flower. I will do this by creating *depth of field*, by blurring the background. I have already put the flower on a separate layer (7). Let's see what happens when I blur the bottom layer. I go to: *Filters > Blur > Gaussian Blur*. I set the *Blur Radius* to 80, and press Enter.

The background is blurred, but now I see a white *halo* coming from the flower (8). The reason for this is that the flower *itself* was *also* blurred, and now spreads out. So *before* blurring, I first have to *remove* the flower. To do this, I will use *Heal Selection*. I press *Ctrl-Z* to undo the blurring.

I *Alt*-click on the top layer to get a selection of the flower. Then I go to: *Filters > Enhance > Heal Selection*. Because *only* the *edge* of the flower becomes visible when we blur, the edge is the important part of the filling. For this reason, I now will set *Filling order* to *Inwards towards center* (9). Heal Selection will now *only* look at the *edges*, which gives the best result for the edges (the *center* of the filling however will be ignored). I click on OK (10). I press *Ctrl-D* to deselect.
I go to: *Filters > Recently Used > Gaussian Blur*, and press Enter. The halo is gone (11).

In the last example we will not look at *large* areas, but at *small* ones. Open *Girl_Close-up.xcf*. I will use *Heal Selection* to remove the freckles from the girls nose. I duplicate the layer, and press *B* to select the brush tool. The brush must be *100% hard*. I set the size to 20. I set the Foreground color to *black*, by pressing the *D* key. I press *Q* to go into *Quick mask mode*. I *right*-click

at the bottom left on the Quick mask *icon*, and I *invert* the visibility of the mask by choosing: *Mask Selected Areas* (12). As a result of this, the *selected* areas will now show in red. This way I can see the face, while I paint the selections in red. All I have to do, is to *click* on the freckles and blemishes that I want to be removed (13). When I'm finished, I press *Q* again to get a *selection* (14).

Let's *hide* the selection for a moment. I can *hide* the selection, by going to: *View > Show Selection* (15). The selection is now *still active*, but the 'marching ants' are hidden.

I open *Heal selection* by going to: *Filters > Recently Used > Heal Selection*. Because of the small selections, I think 20 pixels for *Context sampling width* will be enough. So I type: 2 0, and click on OK. Don't forget to turn the *visibility* of the *selection* back on! Go to: *View > Show Selection* again, or press *Ctrl-H* (*H* stands for *Hide*). Now the selection is *visible* again.

I press *Ctrl-D* to deselect. By toggling the visibility of the top layer, I can compare the before and after. You could also use this method for restoring *old photos* that have many small damages, or dusts. In the next lesson we will look at a variation of the Clone tool, which is the Heal tool.

60. Using the Heal tool

The *Clone* an *Heal* tool differ in one essential way: the *Heal* tool doesn't transfer *Hue* and *Saturation*, but only *Value*. Let's have a look.
Open *Red-green.xcf*. The red and green surfaces differ in that the green (1) has variations in darker and lighter green pixels (so *Value* variations), and the red (2) doesn't have this Value variation. Now let's *compare* the Clone and the Heal tool. I start with the *Clone* tool by pressing *S*, and select the brush with

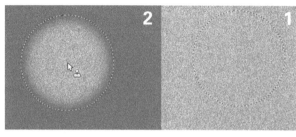

90% hardness. I set the size to about 200.
I take a sample from the green area by *Ctrl*-cliking on it (1). Then I click once at the left, in the red area (2). As we can see, we made a *pure* clone, *Value* included (2). Now I select the *Heal* tool which is placed above the *Clone* tool in the toolbar. It's shortcut is *J*. Again I sample the green area by *Ctrl*-clicking on it,

and I click at the left in the red area (3). The *Heal* tool does *not* copy the *color*, so it doesn't copy the green. *All* that is transferred, is *Value*. Red stays red, but did receive the *structure* of the green. The *structure* of the green is brought over to the red. This is very valuable for retouching, as we will see later.

When I go the other way around, and copy *red* to *green*, we see the *structure* in the green is *removed* (4), because there isn't any structure in the red.

Now let's look at a practical example. Open *Girl_Close-up.xcf*. I zoom in to 400%. I want to remove a blemish. I use the *Clone* tool first. I set the size to 20, and choose a hard brush (to clearly see what happens).
I sample by *Ctrl*-clicking (5), and clone. Because the colors visibly don't match (6), I *do not* want to clone *color*. Now let's repeat this with the *Heal* tool.
I press *Ctrl-Z*, and press *J* to select the *Heal* tool. I sample again by *Ctrl*-clicking (7), and click on the blemish (8). Now the color matches.
I click on the *History* panel. By alternately pressing the *down* and *up* arrow key, I can quickly compare the before and after. We can see the *Heal* tool works well in situations with *color variations*.

In the next lesson we will go a step further, and look at a professional skin retouching technique called Frequency Separation.

61. Professional skin retouching with frequency separation

In this lesson we will look at a professional skin improvement technique, called *Frequency separation*. With Frequency separation you can make skin look *smoother*, without losing the *texture* of the skin.

The way this is done, is by *splitting* the layer into two separate layers. One of these layers will *only* have the *Color* information, and the other layer will *only* have the *Value* information. And it is on the *Value* layer, where the skin *texture* will be visible. So if we smoothe the skin by *blurring* the Color layer, we won't affect the skin *texture*. In the texture, or *Value* layer, we will *improve* the skin texture where needed, by removing texture *irregularities*, with the Heal or Clone tool.

Open *Girl_Close-up.xcf*. I start by duplicating the layer. I name the duplicate: Color (1). I will now *blur* the Color layer. As a result we will *lose all* skin texture. The principle behind Frequency separation is, that the *detail* we lose by blurring, will be *transferred* to the *Value* layer. So from the Color layer, we're *pushing* the detail out, to the Value layer.

I go to: *Filters > Blur > Gaussian Blur*. So how *much* should I blur? A good rule of thumb is to blur just enough, until the *blemishes* have disappeared. If I blur more than that (which *isn't* needed), I will also start to push out *color* to the Value layer. And for a good separation, we want to *minimize color* in the Value layer. I will try 20. I click on OK (2). The Color layer is now ready.

Now let's create the Value layer. To do this, I set the Color layer to: *Grain extract* (3). What we are now seeing (4), will become the Value layer. To do this, I *right*-click on the Color layer, and choose: *New from Visible*. I call the layer: Value.

There is almost no color in the Value layer, which is good.

Now we have a (blurred) `Color` layer (5), and a (black and white) `Value` layer (6). On the `Color` layer is the color information, and in the `Value` layer is the texture information. I select the `Color` layer and set the blending mode *back* to *Normal*.

The last step is to make the `Color` and `Value` layer *work together* as if they were *one* layer. I set the `Value` layer to: *Grain merge*. Now the `Color` and `Value` layer act together as a 'normal' layer. By *Shift*-clicking on the original layer on the bottom, I can toggle between seeing the original layer, and the *frequency separated* layers. Visually, there is no difference.

Now let's start improving the skin. I start with the `Value` layer. I hide the original layer *and* the `Color` layer, so I can work on the `Value` layer. I will zoom in on the nose to 200%. I can see several light and dark skin *irregularities* in the skin texture, that I can remove. I press *J* to select the *Heal* tool. In the *Tool Options*, I select a hard brush, and set the size to 10. I will not remove the freckles now, but focus only on getting a smooth skin *texture*. I will remove the lighter and darker spots. As we can see, the skin texture has become less irregular and bumpy (7).

You could speed up this process by using *Heal selection* as we did before. It's a bit less precise, but you can work much faster. I press *Q* to enter *Quick mask mode*. At the bottom left I *right*-click on the Quick mask *icon*, and I *invert* the visibility of the mask by choosing: *Mask Selected Areas*. I use a hard brush at size 10. I zoom to 300%. I will click on some dark spots (8). I press *Q* again to get a selection. I go to: *Filters > Enhance > Heal Selection*. I will set *Context sampling* to 10 pixels, and click on OK. I press *Ctrl-D* to deselect. I have removed the dark spots. After making a new selection, I can *repeat* Heal Selection *immediately* by just pressing *Ctrl-F*. By pressing *Ctrl-F* you automatically *repeat the last filter*, with it's *last used settings*.

Now lets look at the `color` layer. On the `color` layer I will *smoothe* the color of the skin in certain *areas*, to make the skin more evenly. A convenient way to work, is by using the *Free select* tool. With the *Free select* tool I will drag several *smaller* selections, like this one (9). After drawing a selection, I will *blur* the pixels inside that selection.

To prevent the blurring from being noticeable, it is important that the selection has a *soft edge*. I press Q. As we can see, right now the selection has a *hard edge* (10). I press Q to get a selection again. You can *smoothe* the edge of a *selection* by going to: *Select > Feather*. I will try 40 pixels, and click on OK. I press Q to see the result (11). We can see now the selection has a soft edge. I press Q again.

I can *also* set the feathering in the *Tool options*. I will activate *Feather edges*, and drag *Radius* to 40 (12). The *next* selection I draw, will *automatically* have a *feathered* edge (13). I can't *see* the feathered edge though (I can only see this in *Quick mask mode*). The 'marching ants' will 'walk' through the *middle* of the feathered edge. So I know that the *actual* size of my selection, will be a bit larger than what the 'marching ants' show me. Knowing this, I will avoid coming *to close* to the edges when I draw a selection, because I want to *avoid* mixing skin color with other colors.

To *smoothe* a selected piece of skin, I go to: *Filters > Blur > Gaussian Blur*. For the *Blur Radius*, I will try 80. If I click on *Preview*, I can see the color of the skin is getting smoother (14). I click on OK. Now I will repeat this. I draw a new selection. To quickly *reopen* Gaussian Blur, I can go to: *Filters > Re-Show Gaussian Blur*. The last used value, 80, is still active. I click Cancel. As we saw earlier, by pressing *Ctrl-F* I can *repeat* the last used filter, without having to open the filter. So I *drag* a selection, press *Ctrl-F*, *drag* a selection, press *Ctrl-F*, and so on. I *Shift*-click on the original layer to compare (15).

In the next lesson we will look at a powerful tool for retouching, called IWarp.

62. Liquify with IWarp

IWarp is Gimp's variant of Photoshop's *Liquify*. It can be used for fun, like making someone's eyes really big. But when used subtly, like professional retouchers do, it becomes a serious retouching tool.

Open *Girl_Close-up.xcf*. I go to: *Filters > Distorts > IWarp*. You can make the preview as large as you want by dragging the window out. After *resizing* the window, you can make the preview *sharp* again by clicking on the preview area once, and then clicking on the *Reset* button.

There are six different brushes. One of these six brushes, the *Remove* brush, is a *local undo* brush (1). With the *Remove* brush you can locally remove (part of) an effect you have made before. If you want to undo everything and start over, click on the *Reset* button.

You set the brush *size* with *Deform radius* (2), and you set the *strength* of the effect, with *Deform amount* (3). *Bilinear* (4) needs to be checked, to get a smooth effect. *Adaptive supersample* (5) is an attempt, with extra rendering time, to improve the result. I think that the result is already perfect without it.

Let's start with the *Move* brush. To find a good brush *size*, you have to experiment a bit. The brush size is namely *relative* to the preview size, so with a larger preview, you'll also need a larger brush. Let's try 100. I will make the nose a bit thinner by dragging the left and right nostril closer together (6). With the *Shrink* brush, I click on the end of the nose to make the top smaller (7).

With the *Grow* brush, I could make the girls right eye a bit bigger. To do this, I click on the right eye once.

Swirl clockwise and *counter clockwise* are good for giving *hair* a bit curvature (8).

I select the *Remove* brush (9). *All* applied effects of the area I paint over, will be removed. So if I want to restore the *nose*, and paint over it, I will remove *both* my *Move* brush adjustment, *and* the *Shrink* brush adjustment. I *can't* remove just *one* of them.

For this reason it's best to *save* after a *single* adjustment, by clicking on OK (10), before you make *another* adjustment. Then *reopen* (a copy of) the saved layer back in *IWarp*, and make the next adjustment.

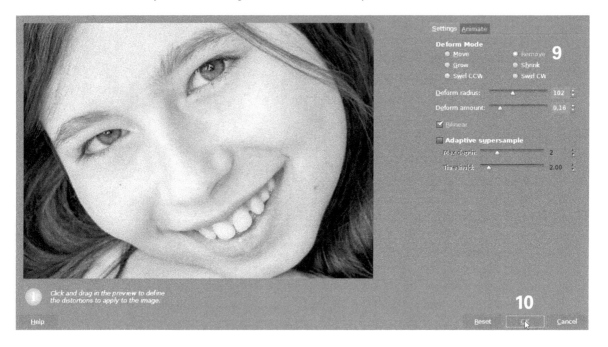

In the next lesson we will look at dodging and burning.

63. Dodging and burning

Dodging and burning is the technique of selectively lightening and darkening an image. When you *dodge* an area, you make that area *lighter*, and when you *burn* an area, you make that area *darker*.

Dodging and burning is often used *after* Frequency separation, for example to accentuate the *contour* and *depth* of a face a bit more.

We've already seen dodging and burning in action in lesson 28 about *layer masks*. In this lecture we will look at another method to dodge and burn. Open *Girl_Close-up.xcf*. For this method I create an empty layer *above* the layer I want to dodge and burn. I open the Color window. I click in the color

square and drag across the bottom until R, G and B are *128* (1). As we see, *Value* has become 50 (2), which means we have a *middle grey*. I click on OK.

I fill the empty layer with the grey, by pressing *Alt-Backspace* (3). I set the grey layer to *Overlay* (4), which makes the grey *disappear* like it's not there.

I press *D* to set the Fore- and Background color to black and white. I press *B* to select the brush, and in the *Tool Options* I select a brush with 0% hardness. I set the size to about 250. I set the brush *Opacity* to about 10%. I paint in the grey layer.

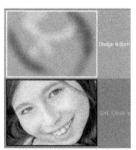

With *black* I can *burn*, and accentuate the shadows. When I want to *dodge*, I simply press *X* to *switch* the Fore- and Background color to *white*.

There are *two advantages* of this method over the *mask* method described in lesson 28. First, there is *no pre-set limit* to the *depth* of the dodging and burning. And second, you *don't* have to *switch layers*, because you're working on only *one* layer.

In the next chapter we will look at how to make a book cover.

Chapter 7

Making e-book covers

64. Make a basic e-book cover

In this lecture we'll make an e-book cover. So what *size* should an e-book cover be? When we look on the Amazon Kindle website, we see that the average e-book cover has an *aspect ratio* of 1.5. This means that the height is 50% larger than the width. And a popular size for self-published books is 6 by 9 inches, which *also* has an aspect ratio of 1.5. So this matches.

Now that we now the aspect ratio, how many *pixels* should our e-book cover be? Amazon recommends for an e-book cover a *minimum height* of 2500 pixels. Let's also have a look at the pixel dimensions of a 6 by 9 inches file, at 300 dpi (which is needed for a printed book). I go to: *File > New*. I click on *pixels* (*px*), and choose: *inches* (1, 2). For *Width* I fill in 6, and for *Height* I fill in 9. I open *Advanced Options* (3), and set pixels/in (**p**ixels **p**er **i**nch, short: ppi, or *dpi*) to 300. We see we now get a file of 1800 x 2700 pixels (4).

2700 pixels is only *slightly* larger than Amazon's minimum requirement of 2500 pixels height. The *advantage* of 2700 pixels is that it now meets the requirements for *both* an e-book cover, *and* a 6 by 9 inch book cover for print. I click on OK.

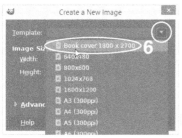

Let's *save* this document as a *template* for reusing. I go to: *File > Create Template* (5). I will name it: *book-cover 1800x2700*, and click on OK. Now I go to: *File > New*, and at the top I click on *Template*. Here I see my e-book cover template (6). I select it, and click on OK.

Now let's open an image that we will use for the cover. Open *Skyline.jpg*. The image comes from a website called *Unsplash.com*. Unsplash offers free, high quality images that come with a *Creative Commons Zero* license. This means: *'you can copy, modify, distribute and use the photos for free, including commercial purposes, without asking permission from or providing attribution to the photographer or Unsplash'*.

6

I drag the image over to my template. I place the image so I see the water and the buildings (6). Now I will place some *guides*, that will help me with placing my text. To do this, I press *Ctrl-A* to get a selection around my document. Then I go to: *Select > Shrink*. I type 250 (7), and press Enter (8). Now I go to: *Image > Guides > New Guides from selection*. I press *Ctrl-D* to deselect (9).

8

If I want to *hide* the guides, I go to: View > *Show Guides*, or press *Ctrl-;*. I can *move* guides with the *Move* tool while holding the *Shift* key down. When I press *Shift* and come close to a guide, the guide will turn red. Then I can move the guide. To *remove* a guide, I simply drag the guide *off* the image. To undo a guide change, press *Ctrl-Z*. To *add* guides by hand, I go to *View > Show Rulers*. Out of the Rulers at the left and the top, I can now drag guides (10).

9

10

The fonts I will use are: *League Gothic* and *Montserrat*. I downloaded them from *fontsquirrel.com* (11). This is a website for free and professional looking fonts, that can be used commercially. The fonts have a *SIL Open Font License*. This means that the fonts can be used commercially and can even be redistributed, as long as they are not being sold. Click on: *Download OTF*. OTF stands for: *Open Type Font*. I open the downloaded *League Gothic* folder. League Gothic has *four* font weights (12). You install a font by *double*-clicking on it. Then click on the *Install* button.

11

LeagueGothic-CondensedItalic.otf
LeagueGothic-CondensedRegular.otf
LeagueGothic-Italic.otf
LeagueGothic-Regular.otf
SIL Open Font License.txt

12

13

To get good contrast for my title, I will use dark text because I have a light background. I select the color picker, and sample a dark blue from a building (13).

My title will be: *Summer in the city*. I will make the word city large. I click on the text tool, and drag a frame on the canvas. Because the guides are *magnetic*, I can now drag the *sides* of the text frame *against* the guides, and they will *snap* like a magnet (14).

magnetic

14

In the *Tool Options* I select the text below *Font* (15), and type: le (16). From the menu I get (17), I select *League Gothic*. I press *Caps Lock* to type with capitals. I click inside the text frame and type CITY. In the *Tool Options*, behind *Justify*, I click on the *Centered* icon. Then, behind *Size*, I click in the text entry field. I press the arrow up key and hold it

down until the text fits the frame (18). If the text frame isn't *high* enough, I'll drag bottom of the frame down (19). When I press *Alt*, I can drag the text frame. Let's experiment with the space *between* the letters a bit. To be able to experiment, I'll create a bit more space by dragging the *sides* of the text frame to the *document edges*, where they will *also* snap.

Under *Justify*, I click in the *Adjust letter spacing* text entry field. With the arrow up key I increase the letter spacing to about 32 (20).

Now I will *duplicate* the text layer. In the *Tool Options*, behind *Size*, I click in the text entry field and press the down arrow key to make the text smaller (to 200). I press the *Alt* key, and drag the text frame up until it snaps against the *upper* guide. I select the text and type: A SUMMER. In the *Tool Options* I select the text under Font, and type: mo. From the menu I select *Montserrat Bold*. I will adjust the size of the text so it doesn't go *outside* the guides. I drag the bottom of the text frame *up*, so the two text frames I now have *don't overlap* (21).

I duplicate the text layer again. I press *Alt*, and drag the text frame between A SUMMER and CITY. I select the text, and type: IN THE. In the *Tool Options* I click in the text entry field, and with the down arrow key I set the size to about 100. I drag the bottom of the text field up again to avoid overlap. At the top, the text is ready (22).

Next I will create a line. I create a new layer by *Shift*-clicking on the new layer button. I press *M* to select the *Rectangle* select tool. I drag a selection *across* the complete *width* of the canvas. In the *Tool Options* under *Size*, I will set the *height* of my selection to 5 pixels (23). The width of the selection is 1800 pixels, which is the width of my document. Now I have a *selection* of 1800 by 5 pixels, which will become my line (24).

To pick a color for the line, I zoom in close on an orange area. I select the *Color Picker* tool. To be able to take the color of a *single pixel*, I *deselect* *Sample average* in the *Tool Options* (25). I click on an orange pixel (26). I open the Color window, and adjust the orange a bit. Now I press *Alt-Backspace* to fill the selection. I press *Ctrl-D* to deselect.

I press *V* to select the *Move* tool, and drag the red line to about the middle of the text IN THE. I zoom in to 200% on the letter E. With my up and down arrow keys, I can nudge the line perfectly to the middle of the E (27). I don't want to see the line everywhere. So I will *hide* the line with a *mask*, and *reveal* the parts I want to see. I *right*-click on the line layer, and choose *Add Layer Mask*. I select *Black*, and press Enter. To reveal the line, I press *M* to select the *Rectangle* select tool. I will drag a selection at the left of the text IN (28). The selection will snap to the left guide. I press *D* to set the Fore- and Background colors to their default. I press *Ctrl-Backspace* to fill the selection with *white* (29). Now I *drag* the selection to the right side, where it will snap against the right ruler (30). I fill with white again to reveal the line at the right side (31). I press *Ctrl-D* to deselect.

At the bottom I will place the author's name. I duplicate the IN THE text layer, and drag it to the bottom. To change the color of the text, in the *Tool Options* I click on the *Color thumbnail* (32). I select white and click on OK. I select the text and type the author's name: Mark Spring. Under *Justify*, I click in the *Adjust letter spacing* text entry field. With the arrow up key I will increase the letter spacing a bit more. I press *Ctrl-;* to hide the guides. Our book cover is finished (33)!

So how will the e-book cover look like on Amazon's website? Before I make a smaller version of the book cover, I will first *save* the document, so I don't lose any work by accident. I go to: *File > Save as*. I name my file: *City-book-cover*.

Now I go to: *Image > Duplicate*. With de *duplicate* I can experiment with the image, without affecting the original. I will start by turning my document into a *single layer*. To do this, I *right*-click in the layers panel, and choose at the bottom: *Flatten Image* (34). All layers have now been merged into *one* layer.

So at what size are the book cover thumbnails shown on Amazon? At this moment, most thumbnails on Amazon are 160 pixels high. To rescale my image to the Amazon thumbnail size, I go to: *Image > Scale Image*. I select the text behind *Height*, type 160, and click on *Scale* (35). I press *Ctrl-1* to see the thumbnail at 100%. Now let's place our thumbnail in the actual Amazon Kindle store web page.

I will make a screenshot of the Amazon Kindle store web page. I do this by pressing the *Print Screen* key on my keyboard. If I don't want to capture the entire screen, but only the *active window*, I hold down the *Alt* key while pressing the *Print Screen* key. In Gimp, I go to: *File > Create > From Clipboard* (36). I press *Ctrl-1* to get a 100% view. I drag the City thumbnail over to the screenshot file, and drag it over another thumbnail, to see the result (37). With my arrow keys, I can move the thumbnail *one pixel* at a time for exact placing.

When you're working on the cover, and you want to have a *preview* of the cover *at thumbnail size* (for example to check the *readability* of the text), you can quickly zoom out, by *Ctrl*-scrolling to *6,25%*, shown at the bottom of the screen (38). The image will then be *168 pixels high*, only a few pixels larger than the Amazon thumbnail size.

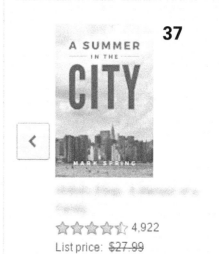

In the next lesson we will make a more advanced book cover, where the focus will be on using blending modes.

New York Times Best Sellers

37

A SUMMER
IN THE
CITY
MARK SPRING

⭐⭐⭐⭐⭒ 4,922
List price: ~~$27.99~~

65. Make an e-book cover using blending modes

For our second book cover the focus will be on the use of blending modes. For our cover I will use two grunge textures. An easy way to find images that can be used *commercially* is to use Google images. I will search for: `grunge texture`. When I click

Grunge Texture Png

Grun

on *Search tools* at the right, I get several extra options. I click on: *Usage rights* (1), and choose: *labelled for commercial reuse with modification* (2). Just to be safe, I will also click on the image to visit the website,

so I can double-check that the image is really 'free' to use. One of the grunge

textures comes from *indiedesigner.com* (3), and one comes from *Aqueoussun* (4). On both sites I can find the *Terms of use*.

Open *kensal_green.jpg*. I will use this image to give *text* a grunge effect. To prepare the image for this, I go to: *Colors > Threshold*.

This tool will make pixels *either* pure black, *or* pure white. By moving the black slider (5) to the left more pixels get white, and by moving it to the right more pixels get black. I am happy with the *default*, so I leave it at 50%. I click on OK. I press *T* to select the *Text* tool, and click on the canvas. I type in capitals: `DEER`. In the *Tool Options* I select the text below *Font*, and type: `le`. From the menu I select *League Gothic*. In the text *Size* entry field I set the size to 1000 and press Enter. To be able to experiment with the 'look' we are going to get, I will use a blending

mode. I *Shift*-click on the create a new layer icon. I drag the new layer on the bottom, and fill it with white (6) by pressing *Ctrl-Backspace*. I drag the *text* layer between the other layers. I select the Grunge layer on top (7), and set it's blending mode to *Lighten only*. Now we can see the grunge effect we will get inside the text (8).

I press *V* to select the *Move* tool and select the text layer. I will drag the text to different places, to see different results. I can also move the text by holding down *Shift* and using the *arrow* keys, which goes fast. And I could experiment with bigger and smaller text to get different results. When I'm ready, I select the Grunge layer. I *Alt*-click on the *text* layer to get its selection. Then I press *Ctrl-J* to make a new layer from the selection (9). I set the *blending mode* of the *Ctrl-J* layer *back* to *Normal*.

Now I open the e-book *template*. I go to: *File > New*. From the Template menu I choose the *e-book template* we made in the last lecture. I press *Ctrl-A* to get a selection around the document. Then I go to: *Select > Shrink*. I type 250, and press Enter. I go to: *Image > Guides > New Guides from selection*. I press *Ctrl-D* to deselect.

I go to my grunge document. I *only* need the *top* layer, so I drag the *top* layer over. The background image I am going to use comes from *Unsplash.com*. I open *Deer.jpg*. The deer image is much *smaller* than the book cover template; it is only *1025* pixels high. To fill the template, it will have to be *2700* pixels high. Because the image doesn't have much detail, it will be no problem to enlarge it. I go to: *Image > Scale Image*. I set *Height* to 2700 pixels, and click on *Scale* (10).

Now that the deer image has the correct height, I drag it over to the template. I will drag the watching deer in the middle (11).

I will now *intensify* the light and the colors of the image with a blending mode from the lighten group; *Dodge*. I create a new layer, and call it Dodge. With the *Color picker* I click on the deer. I fill the Dodge layer with the brown color sampled from the deer by pressing *Alt-Backspace*. I set the layer's blending mode to *Dodge*. The result will be quite bright. To change this, I press *Ctrl-L* to open *Levels*. I drag the midtone slider to the right to darken the result. Now the image has a nice warm *glowing orange*. I also would like to shift the color of the image a bit more to yellow. To do this, I press *Ctrl-U* to open *Hue-Saturation*. To move from Red more to Yellow, I drag *Hue* to the right.

Now I will add a grungy effect to the image.
I open *Metal_Paint.jpg*. I drag the image over. I will *rotate* the
Metal_Paint layer. I go to *Layer > Transform > Rotate 90° clockwise*.
I drag the Metal_Paint layer *below* the *Dodge* layer, and set it to
Overlay. I lower the *Opacity* to about 70% (12).

Now let's include the text. I drag the DEER text
layer we made before, on top. I will color the
black text brown. I go to *Colors > Colorize*.
To turn *pure black* into a color, I first have to
increase *Lightness* a bit (13). Then I drag the
Hue slider to a brown (14). To lose the *white*
pixels in the text (15), I will set the layer to
Multiply (16).

I would like to have a
lightsource shining *through*
the text. Below the *Dodge*
layer, I create a new layer.

I call it Sun. I set the layer to *Screen*. I fill the layer with black (which
won't be visible). I select the brush, and I will paint with white. In the
Tool Options I select a soft brush with 0% hardness. I set the size large,
to 1200. I set the *Opacity* of the brush to 50%. To get the 'shine through'
effect, I will set the DEER text layer to *Burn*. The effect is a bit too
strong, so I will *combine two* blending modes. To do this, I *duplicate*
the text layer, and set the duplicate to *Multiply*. I give both layers 50%
Opacity. I can now adjust the *intensity* and look of the effect,
by adjusting the *Opacity* of both layers (17).

I will also *link* the two text layers so they will move as *one*.

I open the *City* book cover we made in
the previous lesson. I drag the IN THE
text layer over so I can use it again. I place
it on top. I select the text, and type: THE
SECRET OF THE (18).
I select the *Move* tool, and click on the
canvas once. Now with the arrow keys,
I will position the text. I will align the
start of the H, with the start of the D (19).

I duplicate the text layer and type the author's name: MARK SPRING. To set the color I click in the *Tool Options* on the color thumbnail and choose black. Black is a bit dark, so I lower the *Opacity* of the text *layer* to get a lighter tint. With the *Color picker* I now *sample* the color of the text (20). Then I set the *Opacity* of the text layer back to 100%. I *double-click* on the text layer. In the *Tool Options* I click on the color thumbnail again. I select the *eyedropper* from the *Text Color window*, and now click on the *Foreground color*; on the color I just sampled (21).

The reason that I originally used the *Color picker* from the *toolbar*, is that I can use the *Sample average* option in the *Tool Options* (sample an *average* of several pixels). The eyedropper from the *Text Color window*, and the eyedropper from the *Change Foreground Color window*, both don't have this option and will sample a *single* pixel.

In the next lesson we will finish our e-book cover using blending modes.

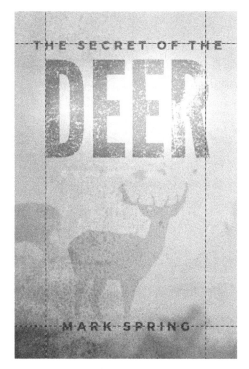

66. Finish an e-book cover using blending modes

Let's do some last adjustments. I would like to lighten up the shadows at the bottom a bit. I duplicate the *Dodge* layer, that I used to lighten up the colors of the deer image. I *right*-click on the duplicate, and choose: *Add Layer Mask*. I select Black, and press Enter. I set the blending mode to *Screen*. I select a soft brush, and set its size to 300. I set the *Opacity* of the brush to 50%. Because the brush will *also* be magnetic, I go to *View* and uncheck both *Snap to guides*, and *Snap to Canvas Edges* for a moment (1). Now I paint with white over the shadows. The result looks a bit greenish. I now select the *content* thumbnail of the layer, and then open *Hue-Saturation*. To move from green to yellow and red, I drag the *Hue* slider to the left (2). I will also increase the *lightness* a bit, and *desaturate*.

To make the authors name stand out more, I will put a lighter box behind the name. I create a new layer below the text layer. I press M to select the *Rectangle* select tool, and drag a box around the text. I zoom in a bit and adjust the selection. I could round the corners, but I will leave the corners sharp. I fill the selection with white, and deselect. I lower the *Opacity* of the layer to 10%. I select the *Move* tool, and click on the canvas. With my arrow keys, I can fine-tune the placement of the box (3).

I also would like to give the text on top a bit glow. I create a new layer below the text layer. I *Alt*-click on the text layer to get it's selection, and press *Alt-Backspace* to fill with white. I deselect. I go to: *Filters > Blur > Gaussian Blur*. I click on the little cross at the bottom right of the preview window (4), and drag to navigate to the text. I can also drag *directly* inside the *preview* window (5). I set *Blur Radius* to 20 (6), and click on OK. I set the blending mode of the layer to *Overlay*.

To make the glow stronger, I *duplicate* the glow layer. I can adjust the *strength* of the glow, by adjusting the *Opacity* of the layer.

Finally, I would like to have some leaves at the top. Below the *Dodge* layers, I create a new layer and call it `leaves`. I set it's blend mode to *Multiply*. I select the brush. In the *Tool Options* I click on the brush icon, and click on the *View as list* icon (7). I drag the scrollbar to the bottom and select *Texture Hose 01*. I set the size to 400, and the *Opacity* to 20%.

With black, I paint around the text close to the edge (8).

I will also manually add a bit of a Vignette effect, making the edges a bit darker than the inside of the document. Below the *Dodge* layers, I create a new layer, and set the blend mode to *Multiply*. I select a soft brush, size 700. I set the brush *Opacity* quite low, to 5%. Now I will darken the right edge a bit (9). Our e-book cover is finished.

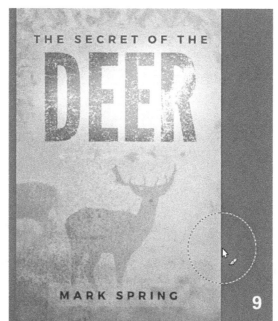

Chapter 8

Gimp specifics

67. Focus in GIMP

In this book I have tried to take away the differences between Gimp and Photoshop. The differences that remain are described in this chapter. I will explain why these differences are there, and how to deal with them.

A difference between Gimp and Photoshop is *focus*. If I click on the *Layers* panel, I can walk through the layers with my up and down arrow keys, to select a different layer (1, 2). I can however *also* use the arrow keys to *move* the content of a layer, as we have done before. To be able to do this, I first clicked on the canvas. By clicking on the canvas, I take the focus away from the layers panel, and *bring* the focus to the canvas. Now the arrow keys behave in a different way; they can now be used to *move* the content of the selected layer.

In Photoshop you *can't* walk through the layers with the arrow keys. Instead, in Photoshop you will *always* move the content on the canvas. If you prefer not to left-click on the canvas, because of the possibility of moving something, you can *double-right-click* on the canvas instead. *Right*-clicking will *only* show a *menu*, and right-clicking again will *hide* the menu again. So *double-right*-clicking is a quick and *safe way* to bring focus to the canvas for using the *arrow keys*.

In the next lesson we will look at the active tool.

68. The active tool

If you *click* on the canvas and a color adjustment opens, for example *Levels*, the reason for this happening is that Levels was the *last used tool*. Let's have a look.

I press *Ctrl-L* to do a *Levels* adjustment, and click OK. Although the Levels *window* has closed, Levels is *still* the *selected tool*, which we also can see in the Tool options (1). So if I click on the canvas, Levels *re-opens* again. Unlike in Photoshop, in Gimp the color adjustments are *also* tools, and can be added in the *toolbox* if you want to. *Like* in Photoshop, a tool *will stay active* until you choose *another* tool.

So when a color adjustment opens after clicking on the canvas, just click on the tool you *intended* to use, for example the *Move* tool, and the color adjustment window will close *automatically*.

In the next lesson we will look at the Floating selection.

69. The floating selection

In Gimp we have the 'Photoshop way' of pasting pixels. If I press *Ctrl-C* and *Ctrl-V*, I will get a *new* layer with the copied content. This is the same behaviour as in Photoshop. However, it is not the *default* way of pasting in Gimp. If we go to: *Edit > Paste as*, we can see in the submenu that *Ctrl-V* has been assigned to *New Layer* (1). It is *not* assigned to the *Paste* command in the main menu (2).

Let's click on the *Paste* command and see what we now see is a *Floating Selection (Pasted Layer)* layer (3). By clicking on the Create a new layer icon (4), I turn it into a *normal* layer (5).

I'll press *Ctrl-Z* to undo. If I click on the *Anchor the floating layer* icon (6), the Floating Selection layer will be *merged down* to the layer below (7).

A *Floating Selection* is Gimp's version of Photoshop's *Ctrl-J*. Let's have a look at how *Ctrl-J* is done *without* the *Layer-via-copy* plugin.

I make a selection with the *Rectangle* select tool. I press *Ctrl-C* to copy the pixels *inside* the selection. I go to: *Edit > Paste*. Then I click on the Create a new layer icon. We now have the same result as pressing *Ctrl-J*. The *difference* is, that with *Ctrl-J* we need *two steps less* to get the same result.

In the next lesson we will look at the Layer Boundary.

70. The layer boundary

In Gimp a layer has a boundary, called the layer Boundary. By default, the layer Boundary has the same size as the image itself. When I make the content of a layer smaller (1, 2), the layer Boundary has shrunken, *together* with the layer content.

If I want to paint or clone on this layer (which I normally wouldn't do; I would use a *new layer* for this to work non-destructively) I see I cannot paint or work *outside* the layer Boundary (3).

I can set the layer Boundary *back* to the image size, by going to: *Layer > Layer to Image Size* (4).

Now I can paint on the whole layer (5).

INDEX

Z

Zoom & Rotate Blur, Nik Collection, 178
Zoom percentage, 31
Zoom tool, 31
Zoom, Fill Window, 130

www.ingramcontent.com/pod-product-compliance
Lightning Source LLC
LaVergne TN
LVHW080115070326
832902LV00015B/2594